The Strength To Serve:

Mental Health Strategies for First Responders and Healthcare Professionals

Tania Bielak, Ph.D

paperback ISBN: 978-1-0697776-0-7

e-book ISBN: 978-1-0697776-1-4

audio book ISBN: 978-1-0697776-2-1

Dedication

To my patients—whose candor, pain, and sacrifice inspired this book.

Table of Contents

Introduction

I have dedicated the last two decades of my career to the care of first responders and healthcare professionals. I have had the privilege of speaking to many bright, talented individuals who chose their respective careers out of a noble desire to help and serve others. Yet, many of them have found themselves in a great deal of psychological distress, unprepared for some of the painfully taxing aspects of their chosen vocations, and struggling to cope with the heavy emotional tolls of their professional roles.

From the experiences of my patients, and from my own as a mental health clinician, I can appreciate the unique challenges of a career focused on caring for and serving others – the pressure to always show up at your best, the need to make quick decisions with potential life-and-death consequences, and the self-doubt and self-reproach that happen when, despite all efforts, suffering continues. Witnessing my patients struggle psychologically after pivotal work events inspired me to write this book. Through sharing these tools and insights with you, I hope this resource will help enhance your self-understanding, emotional strength and resilience, and overall well-being.

You might wonder why anyone would choose to write a single book for first responders and healthcare professionals, given the differences between these occupations. While there's no doubt that the nature of the work within these occupations varies greatly, I have found that the stressors, emotional impacts, and emerging psychological issues are quite similar. It has been my goal in selecting the content for this book that it would be relevant and impactful on folks across all of these professions.

How to Use This Book

This book is not meant to be read quickly. There is a lot to take in, reflect on, and practice. I encourage you to read one to two chapters at a time, and take time to complete the guided reflections and practice the skills. It may be helpful for you to have a journal or a document on your computer where you can take notes and engage in written practice exercises. You can also simply write on the book itself. Please highlight, underline, write in the margins or spaces provided, or otherwise mark up the book in ways that are helpful to you. No need to keep the pages pristine — writing, underlining, and highlighting are great signs that you are engaging deeply with my words and ideas. It is only by thinking, writing, and reflecting on parts that are most relevant and helpful that you will benefit from what I am offering here. I encourage you to revisit the passages that are most relevant to you regularly. Sections that may not initially resonate may feel more relevant later as new experiences and challenges arise in your life.

This book is rich in information across a wide range of themes. Expect that it will be hard to retain more than a few ideas after you finish reading. For this reason, you will find two reflection prompts at the end of most sections, asking you to jot down one or two points that you found especially helpful. Please try not to skip these prompts. Jotting a few key takeaways after reading will make it easier to revisit these key points at a later time without having to necessarily re-read entire passages of text each time.

This book combines two sources of information: my own observations and subjective clinical opinions, impressions, and learning from nearly two decades of work with first responders and healthcare professionals, and the available information and data from scholarly articles and books. Aside from information that has an accompanying citation, the information contained here reflects my current understanding as a clinician working with first responders and healthcare professionals for many years, gained across my work with patients, professional trainings, and reading of the research literature. Given that there is considerable subjectivity within the field of mental health and many lenses through which to view a given psychological challenge, I acknowledge that some of what is shared may not be universally agreed upon. Nevertheless, I have attempted to cover a wide spectrum of issues, and to synthesize my own experiences and the existing academic and clinical literatures into concrete strategies you can readily use in your daily life.

Engaging with this book ideally involves more than just reading. You will be prompted to set a goal at the end of each section. SMART goal setting is a very common behavioral strategy in cognitive-behavioral therapy (CBT). We ask patients to set goals that are Specific, Measurable, Achievable, Relevant, and Time-bound (abbreviated using the acronym SMART). The act of setting and writing down these types of goals has been demonstrated to significantly increase the likelihood of actually achieving them (e.g., Krukowski, 2014). With regard to goal setting, I encourage you to focus on a small number of goals at a given time so as not to become overwhelmed or discouraged, prioritizing those that you believe are most relevant to your current needs and challenges.

As you familiarize yourself with the different sections of this book, take time to notice how the content is affecting you. The strategies offered here are necessarily general, rather than individualized advice for you. You may even find some of the case examples or reflections triggering, or simply not relevant or helpful for your specific circumstances. It is possible, especially if you have been struggling or pushing painful feelings and memories out of awareness for some time, that reading this book may bring painful content to the surface of your awareness. For this reason, before beginning your exploration, consider what resources may be available to you should you become upset by what you read, such as supportive peers, peer support teams at your workplace, an employee assistance program, a therapist, or a primary care physician. If you notice distress in response to what you are reading, or have concerns about any of the content or recommendations and their application to your specific situation, please connect with one of these sources of support before continuing your reading and exploration.

Clinical Examples

I have incorporated numerous clinical examples throughout this book to make the content more accessible and concrete in hopes of helping you, the reader, assimilate it into your own experiences. While some cases are loosely based on individuals I have worked with (often combining characteristics of several people), others are fictional yet realistic individuals intended to illustrate a specific problem or skill. Any identifying information, including name, age, profession, and other specifics, has been altered to protect privacy.

Suicide

Over nearly two decades, I have worked closely with a number of first responders and healthcare professionals who, in their darkest moments, wished they were no longer alive. I have witnessed many times how engaging in therapy, along with other interventions such as medication, spiritual practice, changes in professional or personal circumstances, etc., has helped individuals build a life that feels worth living. Many, when no longer in a dark place, expressed enormous relief and gratitude that their former selves continued to work at healing and recovery and did not give up on life. Many former patients now even use their own past struggles to support others through dark times.

I believe that suicidal thoughts often arise not due to a desire not to be alive, but as a desperate cry for help from parts of us in enormous pain. Patients regularly come to see me believing that suicide is the answer to their pain. I see my job as offering the suffering individual other avenues out of painful circumstances. As a psychologist, I firmly believe it is always possible and preferable to find a path out of our suffering than to end one's life. If you are reading these words, even if you have parts that consider suicide, there are likely also parts of you that want to keep fighting to try and come to a better place emotionally. I hope you will let these more hopeful parts guide you as you continue to engage with resources, like this book, that may pull you toward healing and away from despair. It often takes folks some time experimenting with medication, therapy, and other interventions and life changes before they find the right combination of supports for them. As tough and painful as it is to suffer, I urge you to persist in exploring each and every avenue and opportunity until you find your unique path to well-being. You are worthy of no less.

Section 1:
Caring For Your Body

CHAPTER 1

Feeling "Stressed Out"?

"I think I'm just stressed."

I've lost count of how many patients have come into my office for the first time stating this. Stress is endemic to the human condition, especially in the extraordinarily busy, fast-paced world we live in. But what exactly is stress? How is it different from trauma? How does it manifest in the body and mind? And perhaps most importantly, what can we do about it? These are the issues that will be addressed in this section.

To fully understand stress, let us start with a brief overview of the nervous system. The autonomic nervous system is a part of our nervous system that typically operates in the background, without our conscious control, and regulates important processes necessary for our survival, such as our heartbeat, breathing, and digestion, in response to the demands of the moment. The autonomic nervous system has two main branches: the sympathetic and parasympathetic branches. The sympathetic branch is responsible for responding to danger and threat, whereas the parasympathetic branch controls regulatory functions of the body, such as digestion and rest, when we perceive safety and feel calm.

In simple terms, stress is a state of heightened demand on our bodies and minds. A job interview, a meeting with a manager, or being stuck in a traffic jam can all trigger the stress response. The nervous system detects the heightened demand or perceived threat, and the sympathetic nervous system mobilizes the body's stress response. You might begin to notice an increased heart rate, faster breathing, muscle tension, and a sense of heightened awareness (vigilance) toward your surroundings. After some time, in an ideal situation, the acute stressor passes or is overcome, the body detects the return of safety, and the stress response is gradually diminished with the help of the parasympathetic nervous system. Stress, in and of itself, is not inherently harmful; in fact, confronting and overcoming stressors may even be necessary for growth.

While acute, time-limited stress is common and not harmful, the reality is that many of us face stress that is chronic. Our sympathetic nervous systems are activated throughout the workday by busy days full of demands, difficult patient and colleague interactions, and the pressure-filled, emotionally taxing situations we face, such as witnessing the suffering of others. At the end of the workday, many of us struggle to regulate our stress responses and we may feel wound up, exhausted, irritable, and find it difficult to sleep soundly. We may manage to get some broken sleep, and start the cycle again the next day. Unfortunately, due to chronic stressors and painful events that have not been processed appropriately, the stress response can be activated long-term, a process that can lead to negative psychological and physical outcomes (Cohen, Janicki-Deverts, and Miller, 2007).

In contrast to ordinary stress, trauma occurs when a person is confronted with an event that overwhelms their capacity to cope. Trauma is not just about the intensity of the stressor itself but also the inability to make sense of, integrate, and fully process the experience and associated emotions in a healthy way. Traumatic experiences can lead to lasting negative changes in the brain and body (van der Kolk, 2014).

The Diagnostic and Statistical Manual of Mental Disorders, currently in its fifth edition (DSM-5-TR), defines trauma quite narrowly, with an emphasis on situations involving death, serious injury, or physical or sexual violence (American Psychiatric Association, 2022). In clinical practice, however, the line between stress and trauma becomes quite blurry, as the difference lies in both the nature of the event itself, as well as the capacity and resources of the individual to cope with it. One person might experience a car accident as traumatic, while another might experience it as a stressor. The same applies to encountering a violent patient in an emergency call or in the hospital ward. The distinction becomes even more blurry when there is an accumulation of both stressors and potentially traumatic experiences concurrently, leading to prolonged emotional and physiological stress. This combination is, unfortunately, the reality for many first responders and healthcare professionals whose work may involve encountering the injury and death of others, violence, as well as a plethora of other stressors on a regular basis.

From this point onward, I will combine the discussion of traumatic and chronic stress together as both impact healthcare professionals and first responders. I am not suggesting the two are the same; they are not. But, for those who work in first responder and healthcare professions, I find that there is quite often a combination of the two present. As well, the mental and emotional consequences of chronic stress and trauma can look quite similar, as do the interventions for both. The main difference between overcoming chronic and traumatic stress, in my view, is that symptoms of chronic stress are more responsive to external changes people make in their current circumstances, such as addressing the sources of stress to the degree possible and introducing health-promoting practices, such as improving diet, engaging in regular exercise, and ensuring adequate and restful sleep.

Traumatic stress, on the other hand, is a result of a disruption in the natural healing and recovery process following one or more adverse past experiences. I refer to a *natural* healing and recovery process because the majority of individuals exposed to potentially traumatic events do recover naturally, while about a third go on to develop longstanding distress and traumatic stress symptoms (Bryant, 2013). In traumatic stress, even if we make positive changes in the present, the unresolved traumatic past experiences and their impacts on our minds and bodies can keep the threat response and associated symptoms alive. Thus, traumatic stress requires not only present-day changes, but also work on the emotional, mental, and physical effects of the traumatic experiences on the individual.

This working through of a traumatic experience is otherwise known as "trauma processing," a term we will revisit throughout this book. Trauma processing is a bit of a fuzzy term—there is no single definition for it. What it looks like can vary widely depending on the barriers to recovery in a given person and the therapeutic modality used. Processing may include learning to tolerate memories and painful emotions associated with the traumatic events, examining and reframing beliefs and predictions shaped by the painful experiences, and changing the ways we have coped behaviorally with the painful events to try and re-establish safety, just to name a few. Regardless of the specific approach, the goal of trauma-focused treatment is to promote the natural healing and recovery process and help the affected individual return to a sense of safety and well-being.

CHAPTER 2

Understanding Your Nervous System

When patients begin to understand how their nervous systems work, it becomes easier to manage stress and recover from traumatic experiences. In the following section, we will examine the various states the nervous system can be in under vastly different conditions. Let us first take a closer look at the defining features of each of the prominent nervous system states and the ways they shape our perception, emotion, and behavior. This section draws on insights from the research and writings of Kozlowska and colleagues (2015), Lanius and colleagues (2025), Lang (2000), and Porges (2022).

Safe and Socially Engaged

This is a calm, connected, relaxed state. We feel safe, open, and able to interact with others. Our bodies feel loose and relaxed, heart rate is steady and not elevated, and digestion works well. We are likely in this state when having a relaxed conversation with friends, laughing, making eye contact, feeling present, open, and connected. This is the state in which feelings of love, closeness, trust, and intimacy are most easily accessed.

Fight-or-Flight

This state kicks in when the brain detects danger. It prepares us to fight or run by releasing adrenaline, speeding up the heart rate, and increasing muscle tension. When in the fight-or-flight state, we may feel anxiety, irritability, or panic. We may be selectively alert for any sign of danger or threat, including both physical and social forms of threat. In this state, it may become more difficult to access feelings of closeness, love, and trust toward others.

Freeze

When we feel trapped or helpless and the threat feels inescapable, we may enter a "freeze" response, a state characterized by heightened alertness, stiffness, and immobility. Why would such a state ever be helpful? The freeze response is thought to have evolved to keep us perfectly still, thereby avoiding detection by a predator. This is a state in which both sympathetic and parasympathetic systems are activated. Externally, this results in us being immobilized, but internally, there is a high degree of activation of the stress response. This state is better suited to protecting us from the threats faced by our ancestors than from those we face in the modern world. This is especially true for the situations faced by first responders and healthcare professionals, which call for decisive and swift action, not immobilization. We will expand on this important issue shortly.

Emotional Shutdown

In the presence of a prolonged, inescapable threat, if all other threat responses have not re-established safety, the final stage of the stress response is emotional shutdown. As implied in the name, rather than being an activated state, this state is marked by a dominance of the parasympathetic nervous system, which causes the body and mind to shut down in some ways – heart rate and blood pressure decrease and muscle tone lessens, making it more difficult to generate movement. In this state, dissociation (profound disconnection from present experiences) can play a major role, as there are significant alterations in information processing.

You might wonder why, in the context of severe, prolonged danger, it might make sense for the body and mind to go offline in this way. As described by Lanius and colleagues, this state "allows the traumatized individual to detach from torturous physical and emotional pain experienced within the body during traumatic events" (Lanius, Harricharan, Kearney, & Pandev-Girard, 2025). The state may be adaptive for short-term survival and coping in the course of a severe, inescapable threat. The inherent logic of this state appears to be that, if we cannot physically escape the dreadful situation externally, then we are best to leave it internally, so as not to be overwhelmed by the physical, mental, and emotional pain.

In the long term, however, the shutdown state is associated with a chronic sense of being "dead to the world," being less responsive to both pain and joy or pleasure, generalized learned helplessness, a loss of agency in one's life, and chronic depression (Lanius et al., 2025). In other words, exposure to prolonged and inescapable threat can create adaptations that may be intended to help with immediate survival, but potentially at a great long-term cost.

Put simply, in acute stress, the body mobilizes the fight-or-flight state, aimed at mitigating the danger externally, such as through fighting it off or escaping it. If the threat persists, the body adapts internally to tolerate and survive it, with responses such as freezing and emotional shutdown. These adaptations occur in response to stressors we feel powerless to overcome, and while aimed at helping us survive in the moment, they create lasting physiological and psychological changes that are more difficult to reverse. The focus of therapy, therefore, is to understand, process, and eventually emerge from these threat states in order to regain the ability to feel safe, calm, fully present, and deeply connected to others.

If the nervous system remains in a state of threat, it compromises our capacity to connect meaningfully with others. As Dr. Stephen Porges, neuroscientist and creator of Polyvagal Theory, summarized, "trauma compromises our ability to engage with others by replacing patterns of connection with patterns of protection" (Dana, 2018). In my experience, many health care professionals and first responders find that they spend more and more time in the protective states of the nervous system, due to chronic stress and/or traumatic experiences. When this occurs, it can become difficult to engage effectively and flexibly when spending time with others, or to derive pleasure from situations. It is no wonder that social withdrawal and a lack of feeling pleasure are so common in chronic stress, traumatic stress, and among healthcare professionals and first responders.

I have supported many patients in discovering ways that they can, within the significant constraints and pressures of their occupations, find ways to mitigate the impacts of chronic and traumatic stress on their bodies and minds. Now that we have explored the physiology of stress and trauma, I would like to offer you some practical strategies to help you do the same, based on what has been shown effective in the academic literature, and what has been helpful and effective in my work with patients. This will be the focus of the next chapter

Key Points

What is one thing you are taking away from reading this chapter?

____

Action Plan

What is one way you can develop greater awareness of your nervous system states?

____

CHAPTER 3

Chronic and Traumatic Stress in First Responders and Healthcare Professionals

As mentioned earlier, many healthcare professionals and first responders seek psychological services because they feel increasingly "stuck" in threat-oriented nervous system states. They wish to learn ways to help their bodies return to a sense of safety, calm, and social connectedness. If you struggle to relax and find that you spend much of your time anxious, agitated, or "wired," you are not alone. With awareness and practice, we can learn to enter states of stress when they are needed, but also to exit them when safety, calm, and connection are available. Here are a few practices to help you bring more calm and peace to your nervous system.

1. **Recognize that both hyperarousal and hypoarousal can be responses to chronic stress and trauma.**

   Our responses to threatening situations tend to fall into two categories: hyperarousal and hypoarousal. We are often much more familiar with the "fight-or-flight" symptoms associated with nervous system hyperarousal – anxiety, irritability, restlessness, hypervigilance, and sleep difficulties, to name a few. It is essential to be aware of these states, recognize them in yourself, and learn strategies to manage them.

   However, it is just as important to be aware of and to track the symptoms of the freeze and shutdown states. These are less often discussed in the context of chronic stress and trauma and can manifest in depressed mood, detachment from others, dissociation from one's own body, needs, and emotions, to name a few. These, too, can be caused by trauma and prolonged adversity. Understanding the origins of these difficulties is often helpful in overcoming them. In the following pages, we will explore two case examples of patients working through the process of overcoming hyper- and hypoarousal symptoms.

2. **Use mindfulness to monitor the ways situations and people affect your nervous system. Prioritize safe activities, places, and relationships.**

   As will be discussed in the next chapter, many people cope with chronic and traumatic stress by disconnecting from their bodies. This adaptation allows us to override the cues our bodies send us, such as fatigue or anger, which can help us keep going despite pain and adversity. But this adaptation is costly in a variety of ways, including reduced awareness of potentially unsafe situations. As you become more attuned to the signals of your body using the strategies offered in this book, I encourage you to get curious about how you feel in different places and with different people in your life. Notice whether you feel calm and safe or uneasy and stressed in these situations and explore why. It is important to reflect on why some situations (and people) may trigger your body's threat responses, and consider possible ways to mitigate this activation.

3. **Recognize symptoms of traumatic stress, and seek timely support.**

   For traumatic experiences, even when the event itself has ended, the stress response can remain activated indefinitely, maintained by painful thoughts, memories and nightmares related to the event. It is almost as if this is the mind's built-in way of alerting us to unfinished business. Traumatic stress symptoms may include intrusive memories or nightmares related to an event, difficulties with irritability and sleep, urges to avoid reminders of the event, and changes in beliefs about ourselves, others and the world.

   If an experience is generating significant emotional distress for you, and if this distress does not appear to be resolving in the weeks that follow the event, please do not try to push through or ignore this. This may signal the emergence of traumatic stress. Seeking a therapist's timely guidance in processing this experience is likely to be helpful, allowing your nervous system to re-establish a sense of safety and calm, which is essential for well-being.

It is not a healthy proposition for our bodies to remain in a state of stress activation for a long time unabated, so prompt intervention is key. It is also worth mentioning that, in my experience, it is much easier to unpack and effectively process a traumatic experience that happened last week than a similar event that happened 20 years ago.

4. **Develop strategies to step out of threat states, even briefly.**

   The chronic activation of the nervous system in both chronic stress and traumatic stress erodes the body's capacity for coping over time. Even if much of your workday is necessarily stressful, introducing periods of calm and safety can give the body some helpful breaks from the stress response.

   Some of my patients have put this into practice by starting to take short breaks throughout the day to engage in deep breathing. Others practice a minute or two of mindfulness in their cruiser, ambulance, or fire truck between emergency calls. Others yet take a short walk on hospital grounds. I also urge the folks I work with to eat and hydrate throughout the day to help ensure their bodies are resourced to cope with any stressors that may arise. As we will see shortly, the magnitude of the physiological stress response and our ability to cope with stressors are affected by both the nature of the event and the state of our minds and bodies at the time of the stressor.

   Outside of work, it is beneficial to increase participation in calming, restorative activities on days away from work, such as rest, hobbies, spiritual practice, and supportive, nourishing relationships that allow us to dwell in safety, calmness, and connectedness. It is worth taking the time to reflect on what changes may be possible in your personal circumstances to allow for more peace and calm to be available to your nervous system.

5. **Forgive yourself for the ways your nervous system protects you.**

   Many first responders and healthcare professionals experience guilt and shame when symptoms of the freeze and shutdown nervous system states occur during stressful situations and get in the way of their ability to respond in the way they desire. Whether it is freezing momentarily during a stressful emergency call, feeling unable to respond when being disrespected by a peer or patient, or struggling with motivation and energy to take steps to advance their career, patients tend to become self-critical for not being able to act in the calm, confident manner they wish they could during stressful situations. Ironically, self-criticism is perceived by the nervous system as a threat. As a result, self-criticism for these stress responses compounds and entrenches the nervous system's overall level of stress, worsening the sense of stuckness. This becomes a self-perpetuating cycle that is difficult, to break. Through self-understanding and compassion for why specific triggers register as dangerous and trigger defensive cascades in our bodies, we can practice regulating our nervous systems during periods of stress, gradually introducing the flexibility to respond differently.

Overcoming Nervous System Hyperarousal Symptoms

Individuals who spend much of their time in states of hyperarousal often report feeling on edge, irritable, and anxious most of the time. They often struggle to feel close to others, and the hyperarousal often negatively impacts their most important relationships. Let us consider the following case example: Carlos, a late-career police officer struggling with hyperarousal. This example demonstrates some key elements of the treatment approach aimed at helping a client struggling with chronic hyperarousal find calm, safety, and deep connection with others.

CASE EXAMPLE | Learning to Connect

Carlos was a police officer with over 20 years of experience in law enforcement. Following a particularly stressful time at home and at work, he found himself feeling very restless in between shifts, struggling to fall asleep, and was accused by his wife and adult children of being very irritable. As Carlos learned about and began to track his nervous system states, he found that he was often in the sympathetic "fight-or-flight" state. He was particularly concerned as his irritability (and his loss of libido) were negatively impacting his marriage, with him and his wife feeling increasingly disconnected and prone to arguing.

Carlos began to consciously prioritize opportunities to access states of calm and safety. First, he and his wife began to go on trail walks in the morning hours as they have always found nature quite soothing. He also began to spend time listening to (and singing along with) the Beatles and other beloved bands in his car as he reconnected with his love of music. With some encouragement, he even joined a local yoga studio.

While he was hesitant at first, he agreed to try practicing a mindful body scan several times a week and began to bring mindfulness to the present moment during activities he enjoyed, such as riding his bike on a local trail. He began to notice that, while he used to be alert and on guard much of the time, he was now able to take breaks from vigilance, deriving more enjoyment from activities, provided he felt it was safe to do so.

In addition to these efforts, through trauma-focused interventions, he explored some of the most impactful calls in his history as a police officer, including a call involving an elderly man who died alone and was not discovered until many days after his death. As a junior police officer, this was Carlos's first time seeing the remains of a deceased person in an advanced state of decay. This was a jarring and impactful experience for him. Carlos was able, with the help of his therapist, to access sadness and grief and cry for the man who was essentially forgotten by the world and left to die all alone. He shared that he had not cried in over a decade. Finally accessing and expressing this emotion, which had been with him for most of his career, brought him relief. He learned to access compassion not only for the man's suffering but also for his younger self, a rookie police officer deeply affected by this call.

To his surprise, after months of practicing these skills, he found that he was better able to notice when he was becoming "wound up," to ask his family for space, and to use some of the skills he had learned, such as deep, mindful breathing and bringing attention to his present-moment bodily sensations (sometimes known as grounding) to calm himself. As a result, he became less prone to reacting with anger to family stressors. His emotional and physical connection with his wife began to improve as he gradually became more present and attuned. His adult children enjoyed spending more time with him and have been visiting him more frequently, and he was finally able to enjoy (rather than feel triggered by) spending time with his grandchildren.

If, like Carlos, you are struggling with symptoms of hyperarousal, here are a few activities that you might consider incorporating into your daily life. These have been shown to help regulate hyperarousal symptoms:

- Yoga, Tai Chi, Qigong, or mindfulness meditation
- Self-compassion practices

- A warm, soothing bath
- Swimming
- Spending time in nature (hiking, sitting by a river, etc)
- Snuggling a pet
- Listening to or playing calming music
- Any activity you find soothing and calming

Overcoming Nervous System Hypoarousal Symptoms

In my experience, I have found hypoarousal symptoms, including numbing, depression, dissociation, and pervasive guilt and shame, to be more difficult and take longer to overcome than hyperarousal symptoms. This is not surprising because symptoms of the nervous system shutdown state often show up as a result of severe and/or chronic trauma and adversity. Traumatic experiences in childhood, in particular, are especially likely to create hypoarousal responses to stressful situations (Omidbakhsh, Omidbakhsh, Mohammadi, & Soltanabadi, 2025).

Patients with hypoarousal symptoms resulting from chronic stress and adversity often do not readily recognize the links between current symptoms and past experiences of trauma and adversity. They often believe, instead, that they are lazy, broken, stupid, or simply less capable than others. In reality, their bodies are carrying wounds, traumatic experiences and unprocessed emotions from past adversity, and the symptoms are adaptations to the chronic stress. The physiological stress resulting from the self-criticism for trauma symptoms only amplifies the stress response, in what can become a self-reinforcing cycle.

One of the first steps to changing this cycle is to recognize current symptoms as related to a history of traumatic experiences. To get out of this spiral of shame, helplessness and physiological shutdown symptoms, self-compassion (Chapter 22) serves as an important "circuit breaker" to this self-maintaining negative spiral. By directing compassion to the wounded parts of ourselves that suffered profoundly, and to the parts of ourselves that adapted to survive, we begin to heal, and our capacity to feel safe enough to engage more fully with the world and other people is gradually restored.

Because there is often a history of attachment trauma— adversity related to relationships with important caregivers— in individuals struggling with hypoarousal states, developing relational safety with a therapist and with friends, family members, and romantic partners is paramount. Patients may find themselves drawn to partners and friends who relate to them similarly in some way to the problematic attachment figures, which may lead to re-enacting early relationship dynamics, such as over-giving in relationships or periodically pushing away close others (including the therapist) due to discomfort with intimacy and vulnerability.

It may surprise you to know that you may need both sets of strategies to regulate the body's stress responses, some for hyperarousal and others for hypoarousal. Patients who experience hypoarousal states often also experience periods of hyperarousal, as the nervous system struggles to regulate and can swing between the two states. When one is in a state of hypoarousal, characterized by feelings of being frozen, numb, shut down, apathetic, or dissociated from the present moment, rather than focusing on calming, activities that involve gentle activation of the nervous system through movement and rhythm can be beneficial.

When it comes to accessing psychotherapy, patients with significant hypoarousal symptoms, in my experience, benefit from treatment approaches that incorporate the body directly (known in the mental health field as "bottom-up" or "somatic" approaches). This is because early traumatic experiences are encoded less on the level of the mind and more on the level of the body (Omidbakhsh et al., 2025). Body-based approaches help patients reconnect with and notice the states of their bodies at a given time, as well as tolerate and regulate threat-oriented bodily states. These interventions often incorporate bodily awareness, tolerance of emotions, and gentle movement—a combination that can be incredibly helpful and effective.

CASE EXAMPLE | Reclaiming Safety

Angie was a young emergency room nurse in her first year on the job. She had a history of childhood sexual abuse by a relative, which she endured alone and did not disclose to her parents for fear of "breaking up the family." As the eldest of three sisters, she was also often expected to take on caregiving roles for her sisters while their parents worked long hours to support the family. She had some prior therapy and was generally a very warm, insightful, and nurturing young woman. In recent months, she reported feeling increasingly exhausted, having difficulty getting out of bed in the morning, and struggling to fall asleep between shifts.

Angie was ambivalent about therapy for the first several months. She shared that she found it very hard to trust and be vulnerable. As her trust within the therapeutic relationship slowly grew, she began to share that some of the older male physicians she worked with had been disrespectful toward her, and some of her colleagues seemed to "talk down" to her.

She reported that when she felt hurt by their comments, her body froze and she felt too scared to say anything back. Later, she felt great shame for not standing up for herself more effectively.

Angie's stress was compounded by relationship challenges. Her fiancé, who had indicated that he wanted to marry and build a life together, in practice appeared to Angie to be avoiding discussions about wedding planning, suggesting that he was too busy with work to discuss or act on these intentions.

Angie indicated that, while she knew she must eventually process her childhood adversity to heal from it, she was not ready to broach this topic. Early sessions were supportive in nature and emphasized building a trusting relationship, which was not easy for Angie as she expected the therapist to hurt or abandon her in some way. She was guided to gradually become more aware and tolerant of her emotions and the sensations of her body, including fatigue, sadness, and anger. Between sessions, she started practicing yoga, painting, journaling about past and current experiences, and spending time with close friends. She also joined a martial arts class, as a way to feel more mastery, strength, and control, and less powerlessness in her own body.

Like many early trauma survivors, Angie struggled with self-criticism and shame. Shifting into self-compassion was profoundly difficult for her. In the early months of therapy, she engaged in self-care not because she felt worthy, but due to fear of becoming ill, disabled, and unable to support herself financially. When colleagues were rude to her, she struggled to access her anger and instead felt ashamed that she could not stand up for herself more assertively. This pattern shifted slowly through the course of therapy, as she gradually reconnected with her body and the emotions of anger, fear, and grief.

After many months, Angie stated she was ready to work on her childhood sexual abuse experiences. She shared that it was too difficult for her to discuss the traumatic experiences in detail. She was nevertheless able to work on processing these experiences and accessing self-compassion toward the suffering of her younger self, without being pressured to disclose the details of what had transpired. She started to seek out online content related to childhood abuse and trauma, both by experts and fellow survivors. Seeing that other survivors struggled with similar challenges, she became less self-critical, as she saw the connections between her trauma history and current difficulties, leading to compassion toward herself and motivation to heal. She gradually came to grasp just how much she had suffered during her childhood and how much she had managed to adapt and cope. Above all, she began to see herself, too, as a being worthy of compassion.

As Angie's recovery progressed and as she became more attuned to her body, she began to be more aware of when her boundaries were crossed.

She started letting people know when she was hurt or upset by what they had said or done. Her colleagues began to speak to her with more respect. Many of her relationships strengthened and her fiancé began setting time aside to plan their wedding.

If, like Angie, you suspect that states of hypoarousal may be contributing to your current difficulties, consider engaging in some of the following activities. These have been shown to help regulate the symptoms of nervous system hypoarousal:

- Dancing
- Drumming, chanting, or singing
- Rhythmic aerobic exercise (jogging, cycling, swimming, etc.)
- Gentle shaking of the body
- Bouncing on an exercise ball or trampoline
- Balancing (standing on one foot, using a balance board, etc)
- Practicing yoga or martial arts

Key Points

What is one thing you are taking away from reading this chapter?

____

Action Plan

What is one action you can take to help regulate your nervous system?

____

CHAPTER 4

Disconnection from the Body

Maintaining awareness of our bodies is crucial for effectively managing stress states, and for living a healthy, fulfilling life. Unfortunately, with the heavy demands and stress of work in healthcare or as a first responder, many adapt by becoming increasingly disconnected (or dissociated) from their bodily sensations and emotions. In the short term, this is not only common but perhaps even adaptive.

When waking up at 5 am to make it on time for a 7 am shift, as many of you do, you may notice the body beg for more time to sleep. In these moments, it may be necessary to override these bodily cues in order to make it to work on time. Similarly, when attempting to keep alive a seriously injured patient on the side of a busy road, it is beneficial to be able to subdue, at least temporarily, one's own fear of the cars zooming closely by, and the shock and sadness at the gravity of the young driver's injuries. This adaptation, put simply, helps us to feel less emotional or physical pain, thereby allowing us to carry on with the task at hand. Over time, however, living in this disconnected state can have a variety of adverse consequences.

In the words of neuroscientist Dr. Stephen Porges, "the strategy of numbness has a physiological consequence, because you are turning off the feedback loops between your organs and your brain. So, over time, this numbness works— but the neuroregulation of the organs pays the price" (Hanson, 2023).

The matter is more complex because, for many who become first responders and healthcare professionals, the adaptation of disconnection from the body originated in childhood. Many come from families of origin where their needs were not attended to, or where they had to place the needs of others ahead of their own. While this is not universally the case, many who are drawn to the helping professions do so because the role of helper and caregiver feels "like home". Some may have been given caring roles for younger siblings because their parents worked multiple jobs to make ends meet. For others, it was taking on the roles of a parent who had died or was physically or psychologically unwell. And for many, they served as the family's "peacemaker," emotional support, or sounding board for a parent who needed to feel heard and seen but was not having their own needs met in other relationships.

The Fawn Response

One adaptation that can create a profound disconnect from the body has been called the "fawn response". This involves an individual learning, typically as a child, to appease and please others to avoid conflict or danger. This often occurs in response to inconsistent, impaired, or abusive behavior by caregivers. While undoubtedly protective in the short-term, attuning to others this way and tuning out elements of the self, such as our own needs and emotions, can become a problematic life-long habit.

As adults, individuals who adapted this way tend to describe themselves as people-pleasers. Many lose touch with their own values, emotions, needs, and wants. Their decision-making can continue to be driven primarily by the expectations and approval of others, even when complying causes them harm. Since the need for approval exists on a spectrum (i.e., many of us would prefer approval and validation from others over conflict and invalidation), I believe that this is the is key to distinguishing problematic levels of people-pleasing from more typical ones. Specifically, individuals who regularly engage in behaviors that, while condoned by others, cause them harm—physical, financial, or emotional—can be said to have a maladaptive level of people-pleasing, and in my experience, this is often rooted in childhood adversity.

I have worked with numerous individuals who engaged in problematic levels of people-pleasing, including many first responders and healthcare professionals. Individuals are often painfully aware of their people-pleasing, and many report great shame for this. They are typically puzzled and unsure *why* they do this, and many believe it is because they are simply "weak". These individuals are almost always eager—even desperate—to change this tendency in order to live a more balanced, satisfying life. But, they are also often stuck in a spiral self-criticism and shame for the people-pleasing adaptation. Sadly, this hostile inner landscape creates even more fuel for the need to seek approval and validation— to be seen as "good enough"—in the eyes of others.

If you struggle with people-pleasing in ways that cause you harm, it is important to first acknowledge that this is the case. It is often also helpful, especially in therapy, to explore why you may have had to make this adaptation earlier in your life. This has the potential to spark compassion toward the parts of yourself that adapted this way to survive. For instance, this may be why, despite consciously knowing that self-care is important, you may have really struggled to make space and time to take care of yourself. Many first responders and healthcare professionals who come to me for support report receiving the message that caring for themselves is selfish. Growing up, their worth was determined by their ability to sacrifice and meet the needs of others. To become aware that an underlying belief such as this may be driving your decisions and to recognize its origins is often a necessary precursor to both self-compassion and change.

Whether disconnection from the body originates in your childhood or began later in your life, if you routinely subdue your body's own cues, needs, and emotions, eventually you will likely become exhausted and burnt out. There may be parts of you that are tired and depleted, resentful, and deeply wishing to find a different balance, but not sure where to begin. While it may feel overwhelming to begin to change such longstanding patterns, I encourage you to make this a priority. With the right resources (which, for many, includes the help of a therapist), you can begin to reconnect with your body, and build a life that is congruent with your own values. Suggestions for concrete ways to begin shifting patterns of disconnection will be outlined in the coming chapters.

Reflection

Please take a moment to reflect on your childhood and adolescence.

- Were you expected to take on caregiving roles while you were growing up? If so, what beliefs did you develop about yourself, your role in the family, and other people from these experiences?
- If there were expectations related to caregiving (including emotional caregiving), what were some of your own wants and needs that you had to overlook or sacrifice in order to meet the needs of others?
- In what ways are caregiving or service still dominant in your life? Are there ways in which you currently neglect your own needs and boundaries to show up consistently for others? What are the costs and benefits of this to you and to those around you?
- How motivated are you at this time to make your physical and psychological needs and health a priority? Why or why not?

Reflection

Next, please take a moment to consider the degree to which you may be connected to your body sensations:

1. Do you often struggle to feel and identify your emotions, relying heavily on your thinking, rather than your emotions?
2. Do you often suddenly become aware of intense hunger pangs, a full bladder, or intense fatigue, having been previously unaware of the sensation before it became intense?
3. When you have "gut feelings" about people or situations, do you listen to and explore these, or do you override the sensation and act in accordance with your analytical mind?
4. When you experience pain or discomfort in your body, or illness, do you typically attempt for quite a while to "push through" or carry on? Do you often delay seeking medical support for challenges that adversely affect your body or mind?

CHAPTER 5

The Cost of Disconnection From the Body

The human body is an incredibly complex, sophisticated, miraculous machine. So many separate processes are operating within us simultaneously, in amazing synchrony, and without our conscious control. What is even more remarkable is that this organism possesses an incredible ability to adapt and survive despite changing external demands and environmental challenges—from famine to overabundance, from desert heat to Alaskan cold, and all the varying and ever-changing demands of modern life.

Yet, like any sophisticated piece of machinery, certain conditions are required for the human body to run well in the long term. Since our body cannot speak to us directly, it sends various cues within the body, between different regions of the brain, and between the body and the brain to adapt and meet the organism's present-moment requirements—hunger, sadness, and sleepiness are some examples. In this superhighway of internal information, the vagus nerve, often referred to as the "wanderer" nerve, plays a central role in its processing, guiding the body's autonomic (think: automatic) functions by sending signals between the organs and the brain. Some of the critical bodily functions that are controlled, at least in part, by the vagus nerve include breathing, facial expressions, digestion, and immune responses such as inflammation.

This information guides actions, both within the body and externally, that are appropriate to the current state, maintaining overall homeostasis (which is just a fancy word for "balance") and optimal functioning. The various regions of the body and the brain, under ideal conditions, are in constant, close communication as the body strives to maintain equilibrium and adjust to changing circumstances (i.e., safety and danger, abundance and scarcity, and the complex dynamics of interactions with other people). Through this exchange of information, the body provides the brain with information on what the system currently needs to run optimally. Ideally, this information also helps to shape our choices, prioritizing actions that will restore equilibrium, such as eating when we feel hungry, resting when we are tired, or mobilizing to fight off a threat when attacked.

If we are attuned to what is happening within our bodies—the feelings, emotions, and physiological cues we receive—we can consider this information when making behavioral choices and take steps to help our bodies continue to run smoothly. The disconnection from the body that chronic stress or trauma exposure can generate leads us to override bodily cues and needs (including hunger, fatigue, anger, or sadness), thereby compromising our body's ability to adapt its state to current circumstances. This can contribute to physical and psychological symptoms and, if left unchecked, chronic dysregulation and illness.

Dr. Gabor Maté's *When the Body Says No* is a seminal book that focuses on this issue. Dr. Maté, a Canadian physician, worked for many years in a palliative care setting, where he treated many individuals with chronic health difficulties (cancer, autoimmune disorders, etc). He observed that many of his patients had histories of trauma and adversity and had developed a coping style of being disconnected from their bodies (Maté, 2003). Dr. Maté highlighted a particular pattern of trauma adaptation common to the patients he worked with. He noted a pattern in the histories of his patients where they learned that setting boundaries, saying "no," and expressing anger were unsafe, as these actions risked angering or alienating primary attachment figures. To be clear, this is more than just being nice, agreeable, or wishing to be liked, which are not inherently problematic traits. The adaptation observed by Dr. Maté is a state of such intense fear of disapproval from others that it is the need for approval and validation that becomes the driving force behind most of one's important life choices, instead of these being made in accordance with one's own values, needs, and important life goals.

It is undeniable that this people-pleasing adaptation discussed in the previous chapter, and highlighted by Dr. Maté, helps individuals survive chaotic, traumatic, and neglectful childhood circumstances. But, as Dr. Maté discovered through his work as a palliative care physician, this adaptation often remains with individuals through the remainder of their lives, with health consequences that can be truly catastrophic. Rather than developing awareness and attunement with their own needs, wants, boundaries, and preferences, individuals who make this adaptation are often wired to be excessively attuned to the moods and needs of others (starting with their caregivers). They go on to become adults who struggle to say "no" or set boundaries because of fears of upsetting others and being abandoned. Individuals who have a people-pleasing style often also struggle to differentiate healthy, reciprocal relationships from unhealthy one-sided ones, since they are used to their needs being neglected and expect others not to meet their needs. Many times, they struggle with low self-worth, shame and harsh self-criticism, and physical health challenges as observed by Dr. Maté. They continue throughout their lives to strive to earn the approval and validation of other people, even at the expense of their own health and mental health.

In an interview, Dr. Maté offered the following definition of trauma, which is very relevant to the way childhood adversity impacts attunement with the self: "People think of trauma as these terrible things that happen to you... The trauma is what happens inside of you as a result [...] What happens is a shutdown of the self [...] a disconnection from the body [...] and shame about the self. So trauma ultimately is disconnection from oneself and from the present moment" (Kiloby Center for Recovery, 2017).

These patterns of disconnection from the body to override symptoms of cumulative stress and trauma, or due to an over-attunement with others, as in the case of the people-pleasing style, are protective states I see often in the healthcare professionals and first responders that come to me for help. I suspect that disconnection from your own feelings and needs may be familiar to many of you and may have been with you through much of your life. I also do recognize and acknowledge that for many of you, maybe even most of you, there are enormous current pressures related to workload and workplace demands that are unavoidable and inescapable. There may also be personal demands on you, including tasks of parenting or elder care. Because of these, there may be stretches of time where you may have no choice but to tune out the needs and cues of your body in order to keep functioning in your various roles. There is, however, a huge difference between being in this state of disconnection nearly all of the time, or being in it much of the time but with deliberate, frequent practices of tuning inward.

It may also feel invalidating to some of you to have me suggest that we should adapt and cope mindfully with the stressors we are confronted with, when workload pressures and other systemic challenges keep our days undesirably and consistently stressful. I, too, believe that despite the excellent progress on this in recent decades, ongoing systemic changes are needed to help first responders and healthcare professionals maintain their well-being. I hope that we will continue to see positive changes within first responder and healthcare workplaces that acknowledge the mental and physical challenges that often come with these roles, and which support individuals in maintaining their well-being while practicing within these professions.

While these systemic changes unfold, I hope that the tools I offer in these chapters can improve your well-being, even if the disconnected mode is necessary much of the time you are at work. I encourage you to try and regularly find opportunities to tune inward and meet your body's needs when the situation allows. The goal here is not to become entirely self-absorbed or to abandon your personal or professional responsibilities; rather, the goal is to strike a balance between caring for and serving others, and nourishing yourself and your body. This requires each of us to devote sufficient attention and time to the body (and mind) to maintain physical and mental well-being, a balance which will look different for each of us.

One reason this is so critically important is that disconnection from the body makes it challenging to live a happy and satisfying life. Our body is like a compass. Our body's sensations provide cues as to whether a given decision is right or wrong for us, and these cues may be quite different from our mind's sense of a situation. If we rely heavily on our minds and reason while routinely overriding our gut instincts, we may make decisions that seem logical but are out of alignment with our values and needs. If we are overly attuned to and dependent on the approval of others, our lives may become largely shaped by external demands and pressures rather than our own goals, values, and wishes. Both of these patterns can create feelings of dissonance, frustration, and a lack of overall life satisfaction.

Our emotions and intuition show up in the body. When we are disconnected from, rather than attuned and responsive to, our emotional and somatic cues, we lose this important source of information. We also lose the opportunity to fully experience and overcome positive and painful events. In response to adverse situations, negative emotions such as fear, anger, and sadness are naturally generated, but if we cannot access these, acknowledge and deal with them, they may stay unprocessed in our bodies, leaving us more vulnerable to developing psychological symptoms. On the flipside, when we are not attuned to our bodies and emotions during positive experiences, pleasant feelings such as joy, awe, excitement, connection, and love will also be much less accessible. We may process these situations via the intellect, but it will lack the rich aliveness embodiment and emotions provide.

One common way this shows up in therapy is with patients reporting a loss of interest in and enjoyment from physical touch, ranging from handholding, hugging family members, and cuddling with one's children. This also frequently manifests as a loss of desire and enjoyment from sexual intimacy. These experiences of connecting emotionally and physically with others must be felt directly in the body—the thinking mind often gets in the way. Thus, over the course of therapy, as patients reconnect with their bodies and learn to feel safe, the desire for and enjoyment of touch often reignite, bringing a relief, joy, and a renewed sense of aliveness to patients. Put simply, then, when we are disconnected from our bodies, some of the most meaningful experiences life has to offer become duller and less satisfying.

Reflection

- Can you think of a time when your mind and body had significantly different reactions to a situation or person?
- Which source of information do you tend to be more aware of – your mind or your emotions? Which do you prioritize in decision-making?
- How motivated do you feel to become more attuned to your body and emotions? What aspects of your life might be positively affected by this? Are there aspects that may become more challenging?

Key Points

What is one thing you are taking away from reading this chapter?

Action Plan

What is one action you can take to improve your attunement with your body?

CHAPTER 6

Reconnecting With the Body Through Mindfulness

Given the significant costs of disconnection from the body, I consider helping my patients become more aware and tolerant of emotions and physical sensations one of my most important therapeutic tasks. Patients who have worked with me in therapy will recognize "what do you *feel* when you tell me this?" and "how does this emotion show up *in your body*?" as two questions I pose often. I ask these questions to help my patients develop moment-by-moment awareness of emotions and sensations as they occur in the body. Each time a patient drops out of the analytical state of mind and into their body and emotions with curiosity, the connection between body and mind strengthens, and the dissociative adaptation weakens. The process of becoming aware of the connection between thoughts, emotions, and bodily sensations can be understood as a form of mindfulness practice.

Dr. Jon Kabat-Zinn, a prominent mindfulness teacher and developer of Mindfulness-Based Stress Reduction (MBSR), has referred to mindfulness as developing a love affair with life itself (Kabat-Zinn, 2012). So what is "mindfulness" all about? Mindfulness can be described as the practice of maintaining a moment-by-moment awareness of our thoughts, feelings, bodily sensations, and surrounding environment deliberately and *without judgment* (Kabat-Zinn, 1994). In recent decades, mindfulness, with its roots in Eastern traditions such as Hinduism and Buddhism, has become a mainstream practice and garnered attention for its numerous health and mental health benefits. Practicing mindfulness has been shown to improve mental well-being by reducing stress, anxiety, and depression. Mindfulness can also improve physical health by lowering blood pressure and enhancing immune function (Black & Slavitch, 2016; Creswell, 2017; Goyal et al., 2014; Kabat-Zinn, 1990; Keng, Smoski, & Robins, 2011).

I like to emphasize, especially for folks for whom mindfulness feels too spiritual or religious, that while mindfulness philosophy and practice originated in Hinduism and Buddhism, the way it is currently framed and practiced can be separated from any references to spirituality. I have often heard of mindfulness practice being referred to, quite accurately, as a workout for the mind and brain. In addition to helping us become more attuned to our bodies —a worthy cause in itself —mindfulness is also an excellent way to practice and strengthen the skill of attentional control. In this age of TikTok, social media, constant stimulation via our various devices, and never-ending distractions, strengthening attentional control can be immensely useful for all of us.

With the rapidly growing popularity of mindfulness in mainstream culture, we often treat it as something to perfect and end up criticizing ourselves when our mindfulness experience falls short of what we think it should be. If this is your experience with mindfulness, you may have forgotten a core element of true mindfulness: the non-judgmental stance. I imagine that this is why so many patients have said to me, "I've tried mindfulness, it doesn't work for me!" or "I am so bad at meditation. I guess I am not cut out for this!" For these individuals, mindfulness has become yet another thing to strive for, and another opportunity to fail and experience shame and self-criticism. When patients adopt the same goal-oriented, achievement-focused stance toward mindfulness as they do toward other aspects of their lives, they set themselves up for disappointment and frustration. Being non-judgmental when practicing mindfulness means allowing each practice to be just as it is, accepting that, naturally, some practices will be relaxing while others may, for example, bring painful memories or emotions into awareness. Whether patients are beginning to practice structured mindfulness or day-to-day mindfulness, I ask that, at the end of each practice, they simply take a moment to celebrate and reinforce themselves positively for taking the time to engage in this important wellness-promoting behavior, rather than judging their performance.

As with setting up a physical exercise routine, in preparing for a mental workout involving mindfulness, I ask patients to set aside a small, regular period of time to shift from doing things in the external world to simply being. I encourage them to see mindfulness practice as a time to turn their attention inward and get curious about their own inner world, observing thoughts, emotions, and sensations occurring within them. There are two categories of mindfulness practices that I discuss with my patients: structured practices (such as a guided body scan or breathing meditation) and bringing mindfulness, or non-judgmental awareness, to day-to-day life tasks.

When starting to practice structured mindfulness practices, it is helpful to begin with audio or video guidance with instructions to follow. There are many popular apps and free guided meditations of various lengths that can be easily found online by searching for "mindfulness meditation," "body scan exercise," "walking meditation," or "breathing meditation" in a search engine. The guidance, especially if you find it pleasant to listen to, can help alleviate the mental load of knowing what to do next. Despite having practiced mindfulness for over a decade, I continue to enjoy guided mindfulness practices often, as a way to connect with myself, settle the body and mind during times of stress, and as a break from the busyness of daily life.

As patients begin to incorporate formal mindfulness practices, even brief ones, I also encourage them to bring in-the-moment mindfulness into day-to-day activities. This simply means paying deliberate attention to present moment sensations when performing daily tasks such as eating, showering, walking, or listening to music. It is best to begin with activities that feel neutral or pleasant. When you eat, really taste and savor the food. Focus on the sounds of the music coming from your radio and the sensations of water against your body as you shower. Notice, too, the thoughts and feelings that come up during the activity, acknowledge what has come up, then return to the sensations themselves. For a few minutes, allow yourself to become absorbed fully in the activity, and continue to return to the sensations you are experiencing in the moment. It is not realistic to maintain complete present-moment attention for lengthy periods without being distracted by thoughts, plans, or memories. However, each time we recognize that we have become distracted and intentionally return our attention to the present moment, our capacity for mindfulness becomes a little stronger.

As mentioned earlier, mindfulness has been shown to have numerous health and mental health benefits. A particularly important mental health benefit of mindfulness is the ability to gain distance from recurring, painful thoughts and beliefs (e.g., Chambers, Lo, and Allen, 2008). One common way this is described is that, through mindfulness —the practice of observing and then disengaging from thoughts —we gradually learn to "*see* our thoughts, rather than *be* our thoughts."

It really is a profound change to be able to have the same old thought you've had thousands of times before, such as the self-critical thought "nobody likes me," or the hopeless thought, "there's no point in trying," but to be less and less emotionally impacted by them. This can bring profound change to how we see reality. Instead of automatically believing the thought and feeling intense worry, shame, or despair, being able to notice this thought with calm and equanimity as simply a thought pattern acquired from one's past can greatly improve mental health. It is no overstatement to say that this type of insight can be transformative to our experience of ourselves and the world. The ability to notice thoughts, emotions, and memories arising without necessarily being emotionally impacted by them is a major benefit of consistent mindfulness practice over the long term.

From my experience, mindfulness is perhaps one of the most impactful tools anyone could add to their psychological toolbox. I also assert that it is an especially critical and impactful set of practices for first responders, healthcare providers, and others in similarly stressful occupations. The potential benefits of practicing mindfulness for first responders and healthcare professionals specifically are the following:

1. Mindfulness practices with a focus on the body bring us into greater direct awareness of our body sensations, improving our recognition of emotional states, needs, and boundaries. This is a way of shifting some of the disconnection that chronic stress and trauma can create.
2. With practice, mindfulness can help us calm our mind and body, allowing us to exit the sympathetic nervous system activation and experience periods of rest, calm, presence, and peace.
3. The emphasis in mindfulness on awareness without judgment can make us more aware of our self-talk, including patterns of self-criticism and worry, and their impact on our lives. This awareness is often an necessary precursor to skillful coping and change.
4. Mindfulness is a key ingredient in the crucial skill of self-compassion (Neff, 2015). In order for self-compassion to arise, the first step is to be aware of our own suffering, something that many of us avoid. It is the recognition of suffering, whether in ourselves or in another, that moves us emotionally and motivates a desire to help. Self-compassion, in turn, is a key skill enabling us to process past trauma and to confront stress and adversity in the present. Put simply, without at least some mindfulness, it is very hard to both cope and heal.
5. Mindfulness philosophy emphasizes a stance of non-judgmental acceptance toward reality. Practicing acceptance of reality as it is is

essential for all of us, since adversity, loss, and disappointment are part of our lives. And, for first responders and healthcare professionals who witness considerable pain and suffering by virtue of their work, mindfulness can pave the way to the use of both self-compassion (Chapter 22) and radical acceptance (Chapter 23) in the face of these painful experiences, which in my view are the two most essential practices that help healthcare professionals and first responders maintain their psychological well-being.

To summarize, incorporating mindfulness practices, even brief ones, into one's daily life offers numerous benefits. And for first responders and healthcare professionals, this is one of the most impactful tools for preserving and enhancing well-being. Developing mindfulness can take time, and a non-judgmental, open, and willing stance toward practicing mindfulness is challenging but essential. The following are several informal mindfulness practices to help you get started.

Practice Exercise: Mindful Eating

Eating is an essential activity of life, but we are often lost in our thoughts while we eat. Eating provides a wonderful opportunity to bring mindfulness to a task we must do often anyhow.

To begin, once you have an item of food in front of you, take a moment to appreciate it. Notice the colors, the textures, and the aroma. As you settle in, take a deep breath in through your nose and gently exhale through your mouth.

Awareness while eating

Now, pick up your food, whether it's a piece of fruit, a small snack, or a meal. Hold it in your hands and take a moment to observe it closely. Notice the shape, the color, and any unique features. Consider where it came from—think about the journey it took to get to your plate. You may also wish to generate a moment of gratitude for having access to this nourishing and satisfying piece of food.

Engaging your senses

Bring the food closer to your nose and take a deep breath in. What do you smell? Take a moment to appreciate the aroma and let it awaken your senses. Now, when you're ready, take a small bite. As you place the food in your mouth, notice the texture. Is it crunchy, soft, or smooth? Chew slowly, paying attention to the taste—sweet, salty, bitter, or sour. With each bite, take your time and savor the experience.

Awareness of the body

As you continue to eat, check in with your body. Are you still hungry? Are you satisfied? Take a breath and notice how you feel. If your mind starts to wander, gently bring your focus back to the food and the experience of eating. As you wrap up, take a moment to reflect on the experience. How did the food make you feel? What did you enjoy the most? When you're ready, express gratitude for the food and the nourishment it provides. Take a final deep breath as you conclude your mindful eating practice.

Practice Exercise: Mindful Walking

Choose a quiet space where you can walk without distractions. Stand tall, with your feet hip-width apart. Take a moment to feel the ground beneath your feet. When you're ready, take a deep breath in through your nose and exhale gently through your mouth.

Now, begin to walk slowly. With each step, bring your awareness to the sensations in your feet. Notice how your heel touches the ground first, followed by the rest of your foot. If you are barefoot, feel the texture of the ground beneath your feet. If you are wearing shoes, feel the sensations of the shoes on your soles, ankles, and toes.

As you walk some more, expand your field of awareness and notice your surroundings. What do you see? Observe the colors, shapes, sounds, and movements around you. Let your eyes wander gently, taking in the beauty of the environment.

Listen to the sounds around you—perhaps the rustle of leaves, birds chirping, or the distant hum of traffic. Allow these sounds to ground you in the present moment.

Now, bring your attention to your breath. Notice the rhythm of your breathing as you walk. You might choose to synchronize your breath with your steps, inhaling for a count of three steps and exhaling for another three.

As you walk, notice any thoughts or feelings that arise. Acknowledge them without judgment, then gently guide your focus back to your breath and your steps.

If your mind begins to wander, simply bring your awareness back to the sensations of walking—the feeling of your feet on the ground and the rhythm of your breath.

As you approach the end of your walk, take a few deep breaths to ground yourself in the present moment. Express gratitude for this experience of mindful walking and reaffirm your commitment to practicing mindfulness in this way.

Practice Exercise: Mindfulness of Emotions

The Emotion Wheel below includes many words describing different emotional states. Once or twice a day, you may look at the wheel and ask yourself, "What emotion or emotions am I experiencing right now?" And once that becomes easy, you can add, "What is this emotion trying to tell me right now?"

This is a deceptively simple yet profound practice of intentionally tuning into the body with curiosity, which may, over time, increase your awareness of your body's moment-by-moment states and needs. Over time, you may find that you no longer need to consult the Emotion Wheel to identify what you feel, and that this attuned awareness remains with you throughout the day.

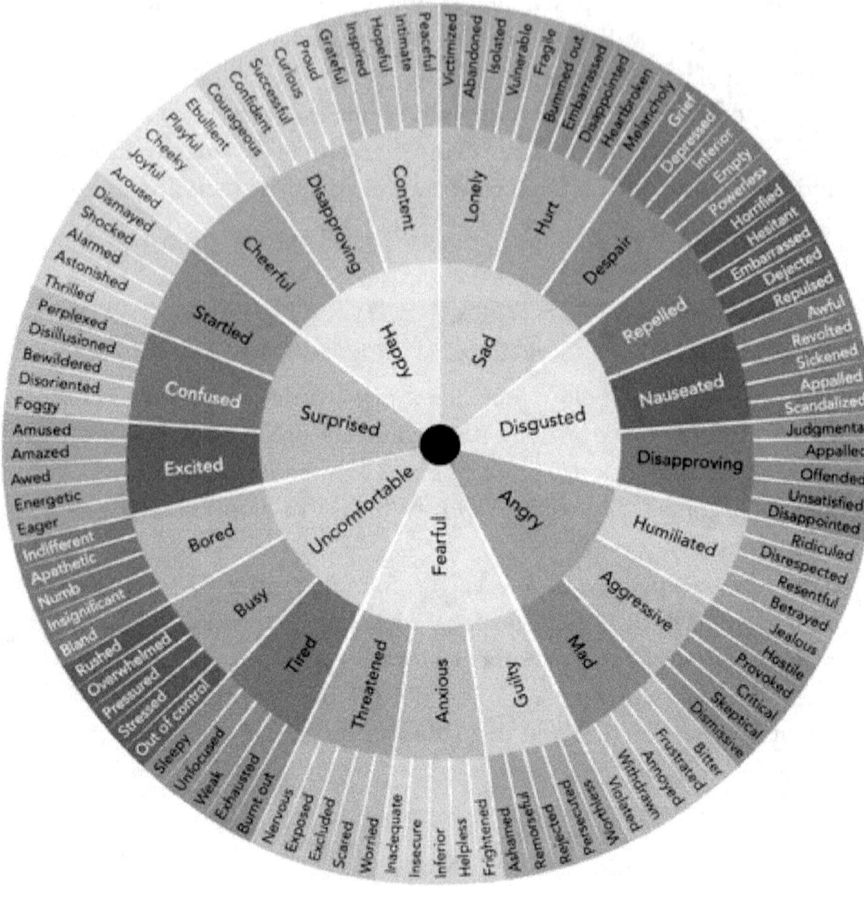

Figure 1. Emotion Wheel, originally introduced by Plutchik, 1980. Adapted by Moran and Ming, 2023. Reprinted with permission.

Practice Exercise: The STOP Mindfulness Check-In

The STOP mindfulness exercise is a brief and informal mindfulness practice derived from Dialectical Behavior Therapy (DBT; Linehan, 2015). When we STOP, we take time to observe our thoughts, emotions, and physical sensations, integrating the information gleaned from all these sources into deciding the best next step. Over time, the regular practice of tuning inward becomes faster and more automatic, and these important sources of information become more readily available.

There are four simple steps to practicing the STOP mindfulness skill.

S	**Stop**	Stop! Freeze! Do not move a muscle! Your emotions may try to make you act without thinking! Stay in control!
T	**Take a step back**	Take a step back from the situation. Take a break. Let go. Take a deep breath. Do not let your feelings make you act impulsively.
O	**Observe**	Notice what is going on inside and outside of you. What is the situation? What are your thoughts and feelings? What are others saying or doing?
P	**Proceed Mindfully**	Act with awareness. When deciding what to do, consider your thoughts and feelings, the situation, and other people's thoughts and feelings. Think about your goals. What actions will make it better or worse?

Figure 2. DBT STOP mindfulness practice (Linehan, 2015). Reprinted with permission.

Key Points

What is one thing you are taking away from reading this chapter?

___

Action Plan

What is one practice you can integrate into your life in order to build a greater capacity for mindfulness?

___

CHAPTER 7

Accessing Wise Mind: The Union of Thought and Emotion

As you begin to bring more awareness to your emotions and bodily sensations, over the weeks and months of practicing mindfulness, a curious, yet remarkably common, experience may arise. Your mind may tell you one thing, while your gut may tell you something else entirely. Although seemingly opposed, the information from our mind and that from our gut can be complementary if we know how to listen to both sources.

Dialectical Behavior Therapy (DBT), an evidence-based therapy modality with excellent empirical support, provides a framework for accessing and utilizing both sources of wisdom. In DBT, the state in which our thoughts and emotions are in agreement with one another is known as Wise Mind. We may notice that we automatically lean toward either logic and reason or emotion in our day-to-day decision-making. Taking time to connect with the two different sources of wisdom and insight can be helpful and eye-opening.

Once we have taken time to collect information from both our rational mind and our emotions and gut intuition, we can begin to look for commonalities or areas of overlap. At times, both reason and emotion have valid, albeit differing needs, and it is possible to pick a "middle way" compromise that honors both. In other situations, we can acknowledge and validate one set of needs while prioritizing the other. As seen in the Case Example below, accessing Wise Mind leads to actions where logic and emotion align, helping us move closer to a solution to the overarching problem.

Wise Mind is not some magical way to immediately solve any problem, but rather a way to discern a wise next step. Learning to act from Wise Mind takes time. When choices and decisions come from our Wise Mind, we may sense a reduction in inner turmoil (or dissonance) that occurs when mind and body are not aligned. When in Wise Mind, we may notice a sense of relative ease and calm, a feeling of having arrived at something that feels right to our core, even if the resulting decision is not "perfect," requires compromise or sacrifice, or results in feelings of grief. Let us examine how arriving at Wise Mind might look in practice.

CASE EXAMPLE | Navigating a Difficult Decision

Susan was a mid-career specialist physician. She had grown increasingly dissatisfied with her current role at a large academic hospital. She described her department chief as being quite demanding, and at times, short and dismissive of Susan's needs and concerns. While she has had recurring thoughts of resigning, she has felt frozen about making these changes, which, in turn, has led to feelings of shame and self-criticism for her inaction.

Susan shared that her analytical mind's position was that she either needs to be more assertive with the chief or resign and find a more suitable role. On the other hand, emotionally, she felt very nervous and was reluctant to commit to change. She was worried about the consequences of losing her job and felt insecure about the future. "Will I find another, better role?" "What impact will this resignation have on my professional reputation and on my family's finances? I have kids that I will need to put through college." At her core, she also doubted her perception of who was to blame for her difficult dynamic with her chief. She wondered, "Maybe there is some way in which I am to blame for how the chief treats me?" Susan also acknowledged feelings of hurt, fear, and anger stemming from her current work situation, and a sense that she would not be able to tolerate it in the long term. With these opposing views from her mind and emotions, Susan felt totally trapped.

As Susan began to acknowledge and validate the different parts of herself, it did not suddenly become clear what she would ultimately do. However, acknowledging these different elements of her position helped her begin to take a more active role in finding a path forward. This included asking for feedback from colleagues about her conduct and that of her chief, beginning to explore the current job market within her specialty, and speaking with her financial planner to understand the impact of a temporary reduction in her income. She first decided to reduce her position to four and then three days per week, which was very helpful in reducing the impact of the role on her. Concurrently, she began exploring options for a new role that may ultimately allow her to leave her current position without compromising her financial security.

As this example shows, listening to our reason and emotion does not typically lead to a clear, immediate resolution when facing a complex situation like Susan's. However, exploring our varying needs and fears helps clarify what the most effective next step may be. As with Susan, this can lead us one step closer to a solution that feels fully congruent to us and meets our needs and values, from both a logical and an emotional perspective.

Reflection

- Think of an issue in your life in which you feel conflicted, perhaps being pulled rationally one way and emotionally in another. This may be related to a relationship, an important decision, or a workplace situation.
- Begin to explore and put into words what your mind has to say about the situation. Examine, also, what your "gut" and emotions say about the same situation. Note, as Susan did, that you may have not one but several rational and emotional reactions to the same event.
- Finally, begin to look for any areas of overlap, otherwise known as accessing Wise Mind. Are there any actions that both your mind and emotions are on board with?
- After each step you take, try to reconnect with both reason and emotion to discern the next step, repeating this as many times as required until you have arrived at a solution you are content with.

Key Points

What is one thing you are taking away from reading this chapter?

____

Action Plan

What is one action you can take to be more aware of and aligned with Wise Mind?

___

CHAPTER 8

Preserving and Protecting the Body

In previous chapters, we have discussed the crucial importance of keeping the nervous system healthy and regulated, and how mindfulness can keep us in touch with our bodies' needs so we don't neglect them, especially in the context of the heavy demands and stressors of first responder and healthcare professions. The body and mind are deeply interconnected, and when the body is suffering, the mind will inevitably suffer too. Even still, it might seem strange that the entire first section of this book, written by a clinical psychologist, focuses on the body and not on the mind. I chose to start with the body because, if our goal is to experience calm, joy, and other states of psychological wellness, investing in understanding and supporting the body is essential to achieving this goal.

I also chose to start with a focus on the body because, unfortunately, the healthcare providers and first responders I speak with often do not prioritize their physical health. I have worked with individuals who have injuries that fester and worsen. Some develop a reliance on processed food or a substance in order to cope with stress. Many have medical appointments that are needed but not scheduled. Many develop a sense of profound resignation and give up on their sleep. I do not judge individuals for this; I have done some of this myself. But I do often worry about the ways these choices can backfire and negatively affect the people I work with and care about. I consider this section to contain some of the most foundational high-priority content that I wish to convey. I hope that through prioritizing this content, I can encourage and motivate you to make modest but sustained changes in how you look after your body.

As a clinician who has witnessed numerous times the long-term consequences of not caring for one's body through my patients, and as someone who has experienced my own set of consequences for the same, I urge you, first, not to fall into the trap of self-criticism around this issue

(Chapter 16). Self-criticism and self-neglect often go hand in hand, and it is not from this emotional state that we become motivated to do better. As indicated above, self-neglect is more often than not an adaptation to stress and unresolved trauma, and if you are neglecting yourself, chances are you may have been conditioned to believe this is the right way to live. Yet, I encourage you, from a place of care, compassion, and a desire to be good to your body, to begin to prioritize the needs of your physical body. True, it is time-consuming and costly to take measures to preserve your health, but it is far more costly and painful to deal with the health ramifications of not doing this enough.

In the coming chapters, we will focus on additional components of caring for your body across several domains, including eating, sleep, addictions, physical exercise, and managing physical illness. I will provide concrete recommendations and strategies that, if you choose to implement them, may help enhance your physical well-being in each of these domains.

As you read the coming chapters, I urge you to consider your current circumstances to determine which changes may be most needed and most sustainable given your current life situation. If you are able to make changes across just one or two of the domains, that's wonderful. By keeping your goals realistic, targeting efforts at the areas of health that are currently most troublesome to you, and celebrating every positive step in the right direction, no matter how small, positive lifestyle changes become likely to happen and be sustained. I hope that these chapters will motivate you to care for yourself while you are caring and serving others, so that your body may unwaveringly sustain you through the coming decades in your chosen career.

CHAPTER 9

Treating Physical Illness

Being a first responder or working in healthcare can create significant physical and psychological stress, as we discussed previously. It is no surprise that physical symptoms often develop in the body. These can be frustrating as they make it even more difficult to function effectively. Trying to balance the heavy demands of work and home life, especially while also enduring pain or other disruptive symptoms, is exceedingly frustrating and challenging. As someone with a number of chronic medical challenges, I can attest to this both professionally and personally, and I can empathize with how tempting it is just to push through symptoms or tell yourself, "it will go away on its own". The challenge is that for many physical conditions, this strategy will not work, as the symptoms require intervention, and left unaddressed, the underlying conditions are likely to worsen.

Many patients come to my office for help with psychological symptoms, but we discover they are also dealing with physical challenges. In the course of the discussion, it may be shared that the client has been postponing the bloodwork their physician has prescribed, has been diagnosed with sleep apnea but avoids using the CPAP machine because it is awkward and noisy, or takes their antidepressant "when I remember to" or "when I need it." The busy pace of life and heavy demands of first responder and healthcare work make it extra difficult to follow up on medical concerns, and systemic issues such as long wait times and difficulties accessing primary care definitely do not help. At the same time, as described in the case example to follow, neglected medical issues often do not resolve on their own, and delays in assessment and intervention can compound the eventual impact.

CASE EXAMPLE | "It's Probably Nothing"

Michael, a firefighter in his 40s, came to therapy for support with work-related and childhood trauma. An exploration of his childhood highlighted significant adversity that seemed quite relevant to current challenges. He shared that his mother had a serious, degenerative physical illness throughout his childhood and teen years. Michael took on caregiving for his younger siblings while his father worked and cared for his mother. When distressed, he would try to cope on his own, so as not to further burden his already struggling parents. He lived most of his young life in chronic stress and fear, and tried to balance all that was expected of him. A bright and introspective client, Michael responded well to psychological treatment. After some months in therapy, I couldn't help but notice a new and interesting pattern. Each time Michael stood up from sitting, he would grimace in pain briefly, indicating that he was experiencing back pain and stiffness. I suggested several times that he get this medically investigated, but he rebuffed it, suggesting it is just a sign of aging. Finally, as the pain became more difficult to ignore, he sought medical investigation and was diagnosed with an inflammatory condition in his spine. He was able to begin receiving the appropriate treatment for this, which is expected to slow the progression, maintain his mobility and vitality, allow him to continue to play sports with his kids, and enable him to continue serving as a firefighter, a career he loves, for decades to come.

As I did with Michael, I often encourage my patients to notice and not ignore new or worsening symptoms, especially persistent ones. Pain, low energy, loss of libido, inability to sleep, and a persistent change in mood can all be your body's ways of communicating that *something is not right,* physically or psychologically. It can be anxiety-provoking to see new symptoms show up, and avoidance and denial can be common ways to cope. I know the struggles of chronic medical concerns both professionally, through many of my patients, and firsthand, so I really do understand the desire to forge forward and hope symptoms disappear on their own. However, while avoidance can be tempting, prompt investigation, assessment, and treatment enable us to understand what our body needs and how we can best support it. I hope that if medical issues arise, you will tackle them head-on and, in doing so, help your body function optimally.

Reflection

- What are your motivations to take better care of your body and health?
- What area of health maintenance feels to be the highest priority at this time?
- What are the barriers that have kept you from addressing these aspects of your health to date? How might you begin to overcome these barriers?

Key Points

What is one thing you are taking away from reading this chapter?

____

Action Plan

What is one way you can better care for your body in the context of illness and injury?

____

CHAPTER 10

Balanced Eating

In my practice, I often speak with busy, depleted shift-working first responders and medical professionals. While I am neither a physician nor a dietician, and so do not make a living designing individualized dietary plans for my patients, I do wish to share with you the set of all-too-common difficulties individuals report in relation to food and eating habits from the point of view of a mental health practitioner. I will offer some practical suggestions based on my experiences with strategies that help busy, depleted individuals eat healthier.

COMMON CHALLENGE: ***I don't have time to prepare meals, so I don't pack enough food (or water), and by the end of the shift, I feel faint, irritable, or "hangry."***

When you are working a busy shift, and if your body is not getting its energy demands met, your body increases its production of stress hormones, such as cortisol, to regulate blood sugar. This is in addition to the cortisol and adrenaline that are secreted in response to the emotional stress you may be facing. Cortisol is a hormone that, while absolutely helpful for the body during acute, time-limited stress, can wreak havoc on the body when elevated for a longer period, leading to metabolic, cardiovascular, and immune system dysfunction, as well as psychological difficulties with energy, mood, and sleep (Jones & Gwenin, 2020; Whitworth, Williamson, & Mangos, 2006).

This is a challenge I myself have faced. In my 20s, as I juggled many years of university study, part-time work, and later the addition of parenting young kids, I would often skip meals or grab a convenient granola bar for energy. I often did not make time for a proper, balanced meal. Suffice it to say, eventually, the stress on my body from these choices caught up with my health, contributing to chronic health challenges. So, while I can empathize with why skipping meals may happen, and I understand that it may be unavoidable at times, I do not recommend letting it become a regular occurrence. It is simply not worth the long-term health consequences.

It is worth noting that when we are stressed and have not eaten for many hours, our body is in a less physiologically resourceful state to meet the demands of the situation, and the overall stress on the body is amplified. Because of this, I encourage you to prioritize, whenever possible, consuming enough high-quality food and sufficient water to get you through your workdays comfortably. When nourished and hydrated properly, your body and mind are likely to reward your care with improved long-term functioning. This is one concrete, attainable step toward well-being that I often find first responders and healthcare workers overlooking.

I can appreciate that it is a real and significant challenge for first responders and healthcare professionals to find time to buy, prepare, pack, transport, and eat a healthy meal. From speaking with many in these occupations, I recognize the multitude of challenges related to eating well that you face daily. Yet, I believe that there are still ways to mostly rely on reasonably whole, nutritionally dense food while at work. Because the specific constraints and challenges of each workplace differ, I encourage you to reflect on what may be possible at your workplace. It is also worth noticing how colleagues and peers who manage to eat healthily do so within the specific constraints of your workplace.

COMMON CHALLENGE: ***I don't have time or energy to engage in meal preparation, so I rely on ultra-processed foods.***

Another common challenge is the struggle to keep up with meal preparation, resulting in convenient processed foods replacing nutrient-dense, whole foods. As a working mother of three school-age children, I can relate to the rushed pace of day-to-day life and the significant amount of time needed to buy fresh, diverse ingredients and to prepare nutritious meals. I often joke with friends that grocery shopping and meal preparation take up most of my waking hours.

I can only imagine that for those of you coming home after working a stressful 12 or 24-hour shift, this is exponentially more difficult. Patients have shared with me that the absolute last thing they want to do after a stressful shift is to run over to Whole Foods and begin cooking. Other patients have told me that while 'on the road' or running between patients on the ward, there is hardly time to take a sip of water or use the washroom, never mind to sit down and eat a meal. I empathize with these challenges and I also believe that each of us can make strides related to dietary habits, within the constraints of our occupation and workplace. The costs of not prioritizing this may not be immediately apparent, but can be higher and more difficult to reverse than many of us may realize.

Highly processed foods are foods that are significantly altered from their original natural source and have many added ingredients, some of which may be linked with adverse impacts on the body. Additionally, during processing, important nutrients such as vitamins, minerals, and fiber are often removed, while salt and sugar are added. Examples of processed food include fast food, hot dogs, chips, cookies, frozen pizzas, and deli meats.

Many of us consume processed foods regularly, both due to their convenience and the busy pace of our lives, and the fact that these foods are, by design, very satisfying to consume. Unfortunately, the more ultra-processed food one consumes, the more vulnerable one becomes to illness, such as cancers, cardiovascular illness, endocrine and metabolic dysfunction, etc (e.g., Bikman, 2020; Lane et al., 2024; Lustig, 2021). There is now also an emerging literature related to the link between diet, metabolic dysregulation in the brain, and neurocognitive issues, such as Alzheimer's disease, as well as a variety of mental illnesses (e.g., see Palmer, 2022).

If your body is currently functional and healthy as you read this, please try not to take this state for granted and do what you can to nourish it well. Changing longstanding, unhealthy eating habits may seem simple in theory, but it is very challenging for many of us. Many of us struggle with our relationship with food, and change is made more complicated by the fact that manufactured (i.e., processed) foods are designed to be extremely palatable for our bodies, triggering reward mechanisms in our brains, (Alonso-Alonso et al, 2015). If you struggle to change your relationship with food, please know you are far from alone. Yet, tackling this challenge is, in my opinion, one of the single most important changes you can make to have a direct positive impact on your health and well-being.

COMMON CHALLENGE: ***Life is busy, stressful, and often upsetting. Food is something I rely on to feel pleasure, distract myself from life stressors, or self-soothe when I feel emotional pain.***

Many individuals feel guilty and ashamed about eating specific types of foods (e.g., sweets, fast food), and these feelings can be stressful in themselves. At the same time, many of us have learned early in life to use food as a readily available way to cope with stress and negative emotions. This can become a spiral that is difficult to break out of – stress and difficult emotions lead to emotional eating of palatable foods, which in turn lead to more negative emotions, and so on. It is very normal to experience pleasure from eating delicious foods, even treats, and there is nothing wrong with this. However, the focus of most of our eating should be on providing nutrition to fuel and nourish our bodies. If food, and particularly non-nutritious food, becomes a frequently relied-upon mechanism for self-soothing and regulation of emotion, it can begin to impact the quality of our health.

So, how do we break the cycle of guilt and shame and find a balanced way to enjoy a wide range of foods while maintaining our health? An important place to start is to replace shame with self-compassion, recognizing that the struggle with moderate consumption of processed foods is extremely common. For patients who eat when they feel negative emotions, practicing mindfulness and self-compassion in the context of negative emotions can reduce the compulsion to eat for self-soothing purposes. For others, replacing food with other experiences that provide pleasure may be impactful in reducing the reliance on food. And finally, by managing the frequency, quantity, and improving the quality of foods consumed for pleasure, one can continue to enjoy pleasurable foods while limiting the associated health consequences.

Here are a few additional strategies to consider to align the quality of your food choices with your health goals.

- **Try to make time for meal preparation on a weekly basis.** Consider preparing easy-to-make, versatile items that can be combined into different meals.
- **Pick simple, nutritious meals based on whole foods that you do not hate.** If something is too hard to make or too time-consuming, or if you hate how it tastes, you are far less likely to make it again. With a little experimentation, you will discover which simple meals are enjoyable, satisfying, and support your overall health.
- **Consider batch cooking on your days off and freezing portions for busier days.** When we are tired, sick, or stressed, we struggle to take the time to meal prep, and we become far more vulnerable to eating what we can easily get, regardless of nutrition. Many also work shifts spaced closely together, making consistent meal prep during the closely-spaced sets of shifts challenging. I recommend preparing large volumes of food when you have more time and having portions that can be easily reheated for times when you are not able to cook but still need to eat.

- **For lunches at work and during particularly busy periods, rely on whole foods that require little preparation rather than processed foods.** Most grocery stores have readily available, reasonably healthy food items, such as rotisserie chickens, guacamole, boiled eggs, nuts, chia pudding, quinoa, salad kits and prepared salads, tuna and sardines, and many other foods that pack a nutritional punch and require little or no prep. During busy times, when meal preparation is not possible, these provide ways to satisfy hunger without compromising nutrition.
- **If you often use food to cope with stress or negative emotions, notice your specific patterns without judgment.** Reflect on what needs you might be meeting (or which emotions you might be numbing) with food. Can you come up with any other strategy to manage these stressors in a healthier way? If this pattern is difficult to break on your own, consider connecting with a clinician who could support you in overcoming this pattern.
- **Make healthier snack foods available to you at home – foods that are both satisfying and have nutritional value.** Items like dark chocolate, chocolate-covered nuts, dates, berries, and other fruits can often help satiate a sweet craving while providing some nutritional benefit relative to other treats. Eliminating the processed foods you have available at home is often also a helpful strategy in reducing reliance on and consumption of these foods.
- **Practice setting realistic expectations regarding the quantity of treat foods consumed.** There is nothing wrong with enjoying treats, but quantity and frequency do matter. Consider (or discuss with a professional) the balance that is most feasible and healthy for you and reinforce yourself positively for sticking to your goals.
- **Reinforce yourself positively for any healthy choice you make.** Behavior paired with positive feelings, such as pride and a sense of agency, becomes more likely to recur in the future. Self-criticism and shame, on the other hand, are not typically conducive to positive, sustained lifestyle changes. Try to pair the behaviors you wish to see grow with a sense of pride for having cared for your body.

- **Consider consulting a dietician or a healthcare professional about eating habits that may be beneficial for your body and circumstances.** If you are struggling with improving your eating habits, consider seeking specialized support. Because food is all around us and we all must eat to survive, making changes to eating habits can be surprisingly challenging, but these changes are possible, especially with professional support, and are worth the effort.

Key Points

What is one thing you are taking away from reading this chapter?

Action Plan

What is one step you can take to improve your eating habits?

CHAPTER 11

Avoidance of Mind-Altering Substances

The following chapter will focus on the role of the three mind-altering substances that come up most frequently in my work with healthcare professionals and first responders. These three substances of focus are alcohol, cannabis, and caffeine. I will also briefly touch on the emerging field of behavioral addictions, an issue that also regularly comes up in therapy sessions. I will discuss the ways each of these substances affects the body and mind, and common challenges first responders and healthcare professionals face as a result of using these substances.

Alcohol

Alcohol is a common way individuals attempt to cope with chronic and traumatic stress, and first responders and healthcare professionals are no exception. Early drinking is often done for the positive consequences— a feeling of pleasure, a reduction in arousal, and when done in the company of others, alcohol is often associated with fun socializing and community building, such as the common act of going out for a beer with colleagues after work. For individuals who are stuck in threat or traumatic stress states, alcohol is often sought after as it provides a reprieve from arousal, allowing access to a sense of relaxation and reduced anxiety, reduced behavioral inhibition, and the ability to have a good time.

Unfortunately, over the longer term, alcohol use is known to actually exacerbate emotional difficulties and psychological symptoms. As a central nervous system depressant, it can worsen depressive symptoms and make people even more prone to irritability and anger. It can worsen conflict and lead to unsafe or unwise decision-making due to its disinhibiting effect (e.g., starting a fight or engaging in unprotected sex). It compounds sleep difficulties by compromising sleep quality. It also contributes to medical challenges such as liver disease an cancers. Finally, alcohol is a factor known to contribute to both suicidal ideation and suicidal behavior, with many suicide attempts occurring in the context of alcohol consumption (Koob & Le Moal, 2008).

Given that alcohol is part of many people's lives, and not always to a problematic degree, it is useful to consider when alcohol use becomes potentially problematic. In 2022, the Canadian Centre on Substance Use and Addiction released guidelines which outlined a low-risk threshold of two or fewer drinks per week, suggesting that individuals try to keep their drinking below this threshold. This is in addition to the directive to not consume alcohol when operating machinery (e.g., driving), when caring for children, if one is or may become pregnant, or for people who are breast-feeding. It is noteworthy that those of us who have been practicing for some time will recognize that these recent guidelines offer a lower threshold for what constitutes risky drinking relative to earlier guidelines. I believe that this recent change reflects the emerging understanding in the medical field that even modest consumption, over time, can contribute to psychological, medical and interpersonal problems.

Cannabis

Like alcohol, cannabis use is prevalent in our culture and growing as its use is becoming legalized in various parts of the world. I have worked with a number of first responders and healthcare professionals who have used cannabis regularly. Cannabis is somewhat less well studied than alcohol, given that it remains illegal (or has only recently been legalized) in much of the world. The situation regarding safe use guidelines is also complicated by the presence of many strains and modes of consuming cannabis, both of which impact metabolism and the potential for adverse effects. The two main compounds of interest in cannabis products include THC (tetrahydro-cannabinol) and CBD (cannabidiol). These compounds impact the body in different ways, and it is THC that produces the feelings of "high" and alters cognition. Cannabis use, in the short term, is known to produce feelings of relaxation, a state that many first responders and medical professionals find difficult to access otherwise.

Over time, however, regular cannabis use has been associated with impairments in attention, memory, and motivation. It has also been shown to contribute to increased anxiety symptoms, and in some individuals, cannabis use can lead to the development of psychosis (Sorkhou, Bedder, & George, 2021).

In 2019, the Canadian government published Canada's lower-risk cannabis use guidelines. The recommendations listed in this document included the recommendation to use cannabis with minimal levels of THC, to not combine alcohol and cannabis, to not drive or operate machinery for at least six hours after using cannabis, and for individuals with a personal or family history of psychosis or substance use disorders, as well as pregnant and nursing individuals, to avoid cannabis products completely (Government of Canada, 2019).

Caffeine

You might be surprised to see a section on caffeine use here, alongside alcohol and cannabis. This may be surprising due to the fact that the consumption of caffeine is incredibly common. Many of us consume caffeine daily in the forms of coffee, tea, pop, and energy drinks, and the potential impacts of caffeine on physical and mental health are rarely discussed. Despite this, I have come across many first responders and healthcare professionals whose caffeine use was a significant contributing factor to their physical and/or emotional difficulties, often in ways that were not immediately obvious.

Unlike cannabis and alcohol, caffeine has a stimulant effect on the nervous system. It works in the body by blocking adenosine, a hormone that causes sleepiness. As a result, we may feel more awake, alert, upbeat, and focused after consuming caffeine. Although it is not often discussed, the use of caffeine is associated with an increased physiological stress response in the body, specifically through elevated levels of cortisol and adrenaline, the same hormones discussed in the context of the physiological stress response (Raza et al., 2024).

Health Canada has offered safety guidelines regarding caffeine use, recommending that adults not exceed 400mg per day. This is the equivalent of approximately two to three cups of drip coffee per day. This is the recommended guideline for the general population, with lower guidelines available for pregnant and breastfeeding individuals (Health Canada, 2025).

As with the other substances highlighted in this section, it is not surprising that caffeine use is so common among first responders and healthcare professionals trying to manage heavy workloads and shifting work schedules. Many use significant amounts of caffeine to try and maintain alertness and ward off sleepiness and drowsiness. However, when caffeine use becomes a frequent coping strategy, and especially if consumed in large quantities, a few challenges can arise.

One of the issues with using caffeine to mask symptoms of fatigue is that it provides a mechanism for temporarily overriding our body's sleepiness cues, allowing us to carry on functioning. Fatigue and sleepiness are our body's ways of signaling a need for rest (and sleep). Overriding this artificially, especially if done frequently, adds significant physiological stress to the body. High levels of caffeine consumption are also associated with an increase in anxiety symptoms and difficulties with sleep. Given that these are some of the most common presenting concerns for health care professionals and first responders, the compounding effect of caffeine use can create significant barriers for recovery and symptom alleviation. This is especially true, as tolerance to the stimulating effects of caffeine is common. Individuals who consume caffeine regularly often need to increase their consumption over time to achieve the same effect (Raza et al., 2024).

Behavioral Addictions

At present, there is one behavioral addiction included in the Diagnostic and Statistical Manual of Mental Disorders, 5th Edition, Text Revision (DSM-5-TR): Gambling addiction. Other behavioral addictions are not yet recognized disorders but are being considered for future editions, including food, shopping, exercise, and sex-related addictions. This recognition of behavioral addictions is a welcome and necessary one in my eyes, as I have encountered many patients reporting struggles with behaviors rather than substances.

In first responders and healthcare workers, compulsive and addictive behaviors can become ways of self-soothing to manage stress, distractions, or ways to feel alive and experience pleasure. And, as with substances, these behaviors can create negative consequences in our lives, including robbing us of time, energy and money we could use for more beneficial purposes, and contributing to physical and psychological dysfunction and problems in relationships. As you review the remainder of this chapter, if you are struggling not with a substance but with a behavioral addiction, consider applying the recommendations offered later in this section to the problematic behavior you are struggling with.

Here are a few recommendations related to mitigating risks associated with the use of alcohol, caffeine, cannabis, or problematic behaviors for first responders and healthcare professionals:

- **Prioritize sleep.** Consider the impact the substance (or behavior) exerts on your sleep, and try to mitigate these by avoiding use for several hours before your desired bedtime. In the case of caffeine, try to replace your use of caffeine with rest or sleep if possible. If you are sleepy, your body is trying to tell you what it needs to function optimally. Do not rely on cannabis and alcohol to help with sleep difficulties, as these substances may help with sleep onset but are known to interfere with, rather than improve, sleep quality.

- **If you are not currently using caffeine, alcohol, or cannabis, try not to begin using them. If you are using them, try not to allow use to escalate.** As discussed, each of these substances can have negative physical and psychological consequences. If you do use one or more of these, keep your use occasional so as to avoid developing a tolerance to the substance, which may prompt you to use more and more to get the same effects.
- **Notice how substances or problematic behaviors are affecting your mental and physical health.** If you are discussing your psychological or physical symptoms (e.g., sleep disturbance, gastrointestinal problems, etc) with your physician or mental health provider, do not forget or intentionally omit discussing your substance use (or compulsive behavior), as these may be contributing to or worsening symptoms.
- **Consider the impact (and potential for impact) of your substance use on your work.** Many services and organizations have strict guidelines related to substance use due to the impact of substances on judgment and safety while performing professional duties. Some workplaces even have surprise drug screenings for their employees. Consider the impact your use may have on your job performance or job security, and reflect on any actions that may mitigate its impact on your work, such as avoiding use on the days leading up to and on the days you are scheduled to work. It may be obvious but it is worth stating that due to the nature of the work of first responders and healthcare professionals, working while under the influence of any substance carries enormous risks to the professional and to the public. If you are struggling to abstain from substance use prior to and during work, please seek support without any delay to ensure your safety and the safety of those you care for or serve.
- **Consider the impact of your use on your personal life.** Substances and behavioral addictions have one thing in common—there is something rewarding in the way the substance or behavior affects us.

Yet, dependence on a substance or behavior can come with important costs to us, in terms of our health, finances, time, and impact on our relationships. It is worth reflecting on what your use provides you (or allows you to avoid), as well as the costs to you of continuing to use the substance or engaging in the behavior.

- **Consider your readiness to address your substance use or excessive reliance on a behavior.** If any substances or behaviors are causing challenges for you in your health, mental health, or relationships, consider whether you may be ready to seek support in addressing these problematic behaviors. If you do not feel ready to seek support yet, consider what would need to happen to make this step more accessible to you.
- **Consider seeking the help of a professional.** Evidence-based psychological treatments can help overcome addictive behaviors, and for some types of difficulties, there are also pharmacological treatments available. If you are concerned about substance use, a helpful first step is to bring this up with your primary health physician or a licensed mental health clinician. They will speak with you about your challenges without any judgment and will be able to lay out the options that may be most suitable for your situation.

Substance Use While Attending Therapy

From the perspective of a clinical psychologist, if a patient is engaging in moderate substance use or a problematic behavior and not currently experiencing negative medical, psychological, or interpersonal repercussions associated with use, the substance use or problematic behavior may still make it more challenging to address and overcome other areas of difficulty, such as anxiety disorder symptoms or traumatic stress. This is especially the case if the substance (or behavior) is being used to self-medicate and manage emotions or psychological distress.

In the context of trauma-focused treatment in particular, the ability to access and tolerate the emotions associated with particular past experiences is considered a central ingredient to healing and recovery in many modalities, as is the development of safer and healthier coping strategies. Frequent reliance on a substance or behavior for the management of emotions can pose a real challenge for therapy to be effective when attempting to recover from mental health difficulties.

CASE EXAMPLE | "It helps me relax"

Eric was a firefighter in his mid-20s. He shared that cannabis had been part of his social life since high school and that it helped him relax. Following a personal stressor, the loss of a grandparent he was close to, and a series of difficult shifts at work, he found that his urges to use cannabis increased and he began to use cannabis daily. As with many patients, Eric had some ambivalence about reducing his cannabis use – it had become an enjoyable part of his routine, many of his friends used cannabis too, and it made him feel more relaxed and ready to sleep at bedtime.

In our work together, we explored some of the problematic ways cannabis was affecting Eric. He started to notice that he experienced increased apathy, hopelessness, and suicidal thoughts when he used cannabis frequently. He also recognized that cannabis made him less "sharp" cognitively, a quality that was important to him. Recognizing that cannabis use was helping him in some ways but harming him in others, he decided to try other strategies to help himself relax and initiate sleep. This included beginning to practice mindfulness and seeking a prescription for a sleep aid from his primary care physician. As he maintained his abstinence from cannabis for several weeks, he noticed that his energy and excitement for life were returning and he was no longer having lingering thoughts of suicide. He still occasionally used cannabis with his friends, but cannabis was no longer part of his daily routine.

I have personally helped quite a few first responders and healthcare providers with substance use challenges to reduce or eliminate their use, and to replace the substance or behavior with healthier coping strategies. Often this results in improvements in both physical and psychological symptoms and is accompanied by a justified feeling of immense pride and accomplishment for successfully overcoming a problematic habit.

CASE EXAMPLE | Staying Alert on Patrol

Shawn was a police officer with 15 years of service. He worked on patrol duties at his local police department and was frequently scheduled to work at night. From the moment Shawn walked into my office, his hyperarousal symptoms were very evident – he spoke quickly, to the point that his thoughts were hard to follow at times. He was restless and fidgety, and he struggled to focus on the things we were discussing. Shawn soon reported that he typically slept only three to four hours per night and has maintained this pattern for years. "How are you continuing to function on so little sleep?" I asked Shawn in disbelief. "Coffee, energy drinks, and working out," he replied matter-of-factly.

Shawn underwent a comprehensive assessment and was diagnosed with service-related post-traumatic stress disorder. While his nervous system arousal was high, it was clear to me that both traumatic stress and the high amounts of caffeine he was consuming were creating the degree of hyperarousal I was witnessing. Ironically, using caffeine to ward off sleepiness was generating more and more underlying fatigue, requiring more and more caffeine to overcome the growing depletion. I helped Shawn see how his caffeine use, while understandable, was contributing to his symptoms. Alongside interventions to address his other symptoms, such as trauma-focused therapy, a gradual reduction in his caffeine use and strategies for improving sleep quality helped Shawn get more consolidated rest. He became more at ease, calm, and focused, and as his body relaxed, his sharp sense of humor came through, as well. He still drinks a cup of coffee on most days and occasionally has an energy drink when needed. However, he no longer relies on caffeinated products to get him through each and every shift.

Key Points

What is one thing you are taking away from reading this chapter?

____

Action Plan

What is one way you can begin to address your substance use or problematic behavior?

____

CHAPTER 12

Prioritizing Sleep

One of the main ways our bodies maintain health, energy, and optimal brain function is through restorative sleep. If our sleep patterns go awry, it can lead to a number of significant health issues. Sleep difficulties are incredibly common among healthcare professionals and first responders, and this is no surprise, given that many in these professions work shifts that rotate between days and nights. For a physiological system that thrives on predictability (they call it "circadian *rhythm*" for a reason), this constant change is a real challenge for the body in the long term.

I recognize that you may not be in a position to change your schedule, but it is still possible and important to take steps to maximize the quality of your sleep. Based on the available research on sleep in shift working professionals and my own clinical experiences, here are a few concrete suggestions that may help optimize your sleep. I encourage you to prioritize giving your body the highest quality of sleep that is possible in your circumstances, rather than resigning yourself to sleeping poorly and being fatigued for the remainder of your working years.

1. **Prioritize consistency**. Depending on your schedule, strive to maintain a sleep and wake schedule that is as consistent as possible. For individuals who work primarily in the day (or at night), this would mean attempting to maintain a fairly consistent sleep schedule even when you are working a different schedule than you typically do, or when you are off from work (Boivin & Boudreau, 2014).
2. **Create a conducive sleep environment**. If you are having to sleep during the daytime, natural light and the noise of those around you are two common barriers that, in addition to your own body, may make it more difficult to achieve 7-9 hours of sleep. Take steps to reduce or mask noise, block out as much light as possible, keep the room temperature cool, and otherwise make the sleep setting as comfortable as possible.

3. **Use light (and its absence) to your advantage**. The human body has used light from the sun (or its absence) as a central cue to regulate the circadian rhythm, and it continues to be a powerful cue to our bodies about whether we need to be awake and alert or sleepy and preparing to rest. If you need to sleep in the daytime when it is bright out, use light-blocking items such as a sleep mask or blackout curtains to block out as much light as possible. Conversely, if you need to wake up and stay alert when it is dark, consider devices such as light-generating alarm clocks or light boxes to improve alertness and reduce sleepiness through exposure to their light (Kaylor, 2025).
4. **Discuss the issue of sleep with those who live with you**. Your loved ones may not understand the emotional and physiological consequences of running on little (or chronically disrupted) sleep. Discuss and negotiate with those who live with you, and recruit the help of your loved ones in ensuring a continuous, uninterrupted sleep window.
5. **Be mindful of the long-term impact of shift work.** As you advance in your career, you may have to make choices among various roles and schedules. You may find yourself in a position to have more choice with regard to your role and working hours. I encourage you to prioritize roles and schedules that allow for as much consistency as possible in your sleep schedule, as the physiological risks of shift work worsen the longer we do it.
6. **Practice other healthy lifestyle habits**. Shiftwork, especially with shifts that frequently change from days to nights, is very tough on the body. While this may be a necessary aspect of your chosen career, I encourage you to prioritize maximizing the sleep quality you are able to get under the given circumstances. I also encourage you to compensate for this chronic stressor by taking care of your body in other ways, such as healthy eating, mindfulness practice, nourishing relationships, etc. This could help reduce overall risk through actions that are well within your direct control.
7. **Do not resign yourself to poor sleep in the long term.** Seek professional support to achieve consistent, restorative sleep. If the other strategies have not proven sufficient and your sleep continues to be suboptimal, discuss options with your primary healthcare provider. Some of my patients who are long-term shift-working professionals

do require the assistance of their medical or mental health practitioners to regulate their sleep, including through medication. Many of my patients have attempted instead to address longstanding sleep challenges with over-the-counter medication, cannabis, energy drinks or coffee, and other strategies. However, these strategies are not helpful in the long term and tend to backfire. Instead of coping this way, if sleep is an ongoing struggle for you, please discuss your sleep struggles with your primary healthcare provider or with a qualified mental health clinician, who should be able to help identify and address your specific barriers to restful sleep. Please do not give up on restful sleep or convince yourself that sleep is an optional luxury. It is not. It is a foundational physical need for physical and mental health maintenance in the long-term. While this is certainly more difficult when working shiftwork, it is still possible for most people with the right supports, strategies and interventions to obtain adequate sleep at least most of the time.

It is noteworthy that, over the course of therapy, through interventions such as processing traumatic experiences, increasing physical exercise, setting boundaries, and improving relationships, among others, people often find that their sleep quality improves alongside other symptoms. Thus, if you are struggling with your sleep, a combination of interventions that target sleep and work on other aspects of physical and mental health can often combine to offer the best overall improvement in sleep quality.

Obstructive Sleep Apnea

Many healthcare professionals and first responders who come to see me discover over the course of their treatment that they have obstructive sleep apnea, which is a condition requiring medical assessment and intervention. Research has shown a strong association between traumatic stress symptoms and obstructive sleep apnea (Shah et al. 2024).

Untreated sleep apnea not only saps sleep quality but can also have negative long-term health consequences (Golbidi et al., 2012). As a result of its prevalence, I encourage my patients who struggle with sleep in the long term to undergo a sleep study to rule out sleep apnea, which they are often reluctant to do. To the surprise and disappointment of many patients, the results often confirm the presence of sleep apnea. While patients are often understandably disappointed to find they have this condition, and are far from eager to begin to use the CPAP or other recommended treatments, once the condition is medically addressed, their sleep and energy tend to improve significantly, and they become grateful that this issue was identified and addressed, and that they can now sleep soundly once again.

Key Points

What is one thing you are taking away from reading this chapter?

Action Plan

What is one way you can begin to improve the quality of your sleep?

CHAPTER 13

Physical Exercise

It will likely not surprise you to read that physical exercise is a crucial way to maintain psychological and physical wellness, and to cope with stress, anxiety, and trauma symptoms. I would go so far as to say that if you currently do not exercise regularly, changing this one behavior is very likely to yield positive mental health benefits, perhaps faster than any other behavioral change (the exception, of course, is beginning to take medication).

Physical exercise is a crucial element in the coping and resilience for many first responders and healthcare professionals I have worked with. It is one of the few behaviors that has a significant role in maintaining both physical and psychological well-being. One of the reasons exercise is so important is its role in helping us regulate our nervous system activation. For many, it is a way to shift out of threat-oriented nervous system states (e.g., fight-or-flight) and into a more present, relaxed physiological state. Physical activity has been shown to have such a robust positive impact on mood and on anxiety symptoms, in particular, that some even consider it a first-line treatment for mild-to-moderate mood and anxiety disorders, with similar impact on symptoms as medication and psychotherapy (e.g., see Carek et al., 2011).

Exercise is crucially important to our mental and physical well-being. We've all likely had the experience of feeling increased aliveness, energy, and motivation after a good run or a workout. Yet, if you have had difficulty finding time and energy to incorporate *regular* exercise into your busy life, you are far from alone. Knowing something is beneficial is one thing; being deliberate in making time and space for it on a regular basis is another thing entirely. But I believe that, given the chronic stress many healthcare providers and first responders experience, physical exercise has tremendous untapped potential to deliver a number of distinct benefits, including regulating the nervous system, increasing insulin sensitivity, improving mood, and regulating sleep, just to name a few.

Having said all this, many of my patients were not physically active in the months leading up to working together. This can be due to the busy pace of life, not having found an activity they enjoy and can regularly engage in, physical pain or injury, or simply feeling chronically exhausted. There are also a couple of common pitfalls that often occur when individuals attempt to start exercising after a period of inactivity, which can interfere with making this a sustainable and consistent part of their self-care routine.

First, if you have been fit and active in the past but are not currently, attempting to re-engage with fitness can, for many, trigger self-criticism and shame. You might begin to compare your current abilities with what your stronger, faster prior self was capable of. It is not unusual to begin exercising, an important step toward improved health, yet to feel dejected and ashamed as a result of the relentless self-criticism. People can often become very impatient with themselves and their bodies, setting unrealistically high goals and expectations for themselves, related to frequency or intensity of exercise, and especially related to weight loss. This almost invariably sets them up for failure and disappointment when they begin a wonderful new habit, but are unable to keep up with or achieve their own goals.

If you are serious about wanting to begin exercising, that's really wonderful and I congratulate you. Exercise is a major source of resilience in my own life, and I believe it can be a source of well-being for you as well. Here are some concrete steps that may help you become more active:

1. **Select an activity that you are likely to enjoy (or at least not one you hate doing).** Some people love exercising with groups, others alone. Some people like to go to the gym, while others exercise at home, play sports, or exercise outdoors. If you are unsure what you might enjoy, I recommend experimenting with different settings and types of exercise to see what feels good to you both physically and emotionally.

2. **Set modest, realistic goals that are attainable and sustainable given your current fitness level and life constraints.** Being realistic with yourself and setting yourself up to experience success is one way to ensure that exercise will be associated with positive, rather than negative, emotions. This will make it more likely that your motivation to continue will increase, rather than fizzle out.

3. **Remember the old saying, "Rome was not built in a day," and keep your goals realistic and modest.** I have had more than one client become overzealous in beginning to work out, and either become discouraged for not being able to maintain the intensity, or

sustain an injury, and become unable to work out for a long time. Please be patient with your body as you build strength and endurance, be mindful of maintaining proper form, and respect any limitations due to injuries you may have. If you have any medical conditions or past injuries, speaking to your primary healthcare provider can ensure that exercise is done safely and within your body's current limits. If you have any concerns about how your body is responding to exercise, please do not ignore pain or discomfort and consult with your physician before continuing. Having someone to guide you, such as a trainer, may help you get started and ensure you are exercising safely.

4. **Orient your motivation for exercise toward health and well-being, and away from body shape and weight**. Many people exercise for the primary goal of achieving a certain weight or size, and become quickly disappointed and demotivated when this goal is not met. Some of us could use losing some weight for optimal health. Yet, many factors influence our weight and body shape, including genetics, stress levels, sleep patterns, age, hormones, and medication, among others. Because weight is affected by many factors we cannot control, I encourage patients to focus instead on the health benefits of exercise – building muscle mass, improving bone density, enhancing cardiovascular health, stress management, and mood-related benefits. Focusing on weight loss as the primary motivation for exercising can quickly become disappointing and discouraging when results are not forthcoming. On a related note, it is worth recognizing and accepting that the weight at which your body functions best may not be the size and shape you would choose for yourself.

5. **Ensure that exercise becomes a positive experience and a source of positive self-talk and emotions.** Reframe or disengage from unhelpful thinking patterns, such as self-criticism for not being fit "enough". Ensure that your self-talk is oriented toward reinforcing consistency rather than judging performance or body weight. If you find yourself harboring harsh self-judgments about your exercise performance or level of fitness, this is an opportunity to incorporate several of the tools recommended throughout this book, including identifying and challenging unhelpful thinking styles (Chapter 15), practicing radical acceptance (Chapter 23), and cultivating self-compassion (Chapter 22). If you are able to generate praise for yourself

using self-talk such as, "What a great step I am taking by choosing to care for my body in this way," or "My body feels so relaxed and at ease after a good run," you increase the likelihood of becoming motivated to exercise again. Over time, these positive, incremental changes in strength, endurance, and mental health are likely to keep your momentum going. Exercise is a tough one to stick with for many of us, but don't give up; your body is counting on you to provide it with the movement it needs to thrive.

Key Points

What is one thing you are taking away from reading this chapter?

____

Action Plan

What is one action you can take to increase your physical fitness through movement?

____

SECTION 2:
CARING FOR YOUR MIND

CHAPTER 14

'Thinking Traps': Negative Automatic Thoughts

How we make sense of life events has an enormous impact on our experience of our lives. This is one of the core premises of CBT (cognitive behavioral therapy), a frontline evidence-based treatment for many types of psychological difficulties, including depression, anxiety, and traumatic stress disorders. When patients come to therapy, they often learn to monitor their habitual thinking patterns and identify unhelpful thinking styles, which are otherwise known as "thinking traps". There are quite a few common thinking traps. I have identified five common thinking traps that often cause problems for first responders and healthcare professionals, and I wish to share them with you.

1. **All-or-Nothing or Black-and-White Reasoning**: A tendency to evaluate situations, people, or oneself as either "this" or "that," leaving little room for nuance.

   Case Example: Pierce, a late-career physician, is frequently frustrated with other people. He has a tendency to evaluate other hospital staff as completely incompetent, hospital administrators as totally unsupportive and disinterested in his well-being, and patients as uniformly entitled and unreasonable. He is considering an early retirement as he becomes increasingly dissatisfied with his work.

   Black and white thinking is problematic because, when we think in extreme ways, we lose access to information that adds nuance to our view of the situation. We may only see one side of a situation and may be blinded by past experiences and feelings. This can lead to increased feelings of anger, helplessness, and hopelessness, and a reduced capacity for effective problem-solving.

2. **Catastrophizing**: Predicting the worst possible outcome, and believing this to be more probable than it is in reality.

   Case Example: Cindy and her husband, Robert, were on the market for a new home. As the parents of two young boys, 2 and 6 years old, Robert was excited about the prospect of a home with a pool in the backyard. Cindy, however, wouldn't even consider it. As a paramedic, she has seen too many times how quickly a young child can drown in a backyard pool. She couldn't bear the thought of this happening to her boys.

   Many first responders and healthcare professionals, by virtue of frequent exposure to tragic situations involving accidental and/or violent injury or death, become quite worried about the safety of their loved ones. In particular, patients with young children may resort to over-protective behaviors (also known as "safety behaviors") to help manage their anxiety and worry.

   As implied in the example above, a tendency to engage in catastrophic thinking contributes to worry and anxiety symptoms and can be emotionally and physiologically depleting. While awareness of danger is useful, an overestimation of danger may lead to hypervigilance, persistent anxiety, and hyperarousal symptoms (e.g., tension in the body, difficulty concentrating, insomnia, irritability). This way of thinking can contribute to avoidance behaviors. Being in an anxious, vigilant state much of the time also diminishes our capacity for presence and for positive emotions, such as trust, happiness, and closeness with others.

3. **Mind Reading:** Believing that we know what someone else is thinking or feeling without sufficient information.

   Case Example: David, an early-career firefighter, attended his first suicide-by-hanging call. While he was still able to complete all aspects of the call, he left the call with strong feelings of anxiety and shame, believing that his partner and other personnel on the scene (e.g., police officers) were judging him for his shaking hands and trembling voice, and for taking "too long" to complete tasks.

   Many individuals in first responder and healthcare occupations have a tendency to expect and perceive negative evaluations by others, a tendency that often predates their taking on their respective professional roles. This is compounded by the fact that evaluation is inherent in the training to become either a healthcare provider or a first responder (e.g., preceptorships, residency). Throughout their careers, individuals have to perform difficult, time-sensitive tasks in the company of colleagues, mentors, other professionals and members of the public. Believing frequently that you are being negatively evaluated by others is a pernicious psychological habit that can amplify anxiety, shame, and feelings of low self-worth and make it more difficult to connect authentically with other people.

4. **Should Statements: "Should" thinking is a person's imposing of their own expectations** or standards on reality, on others, and on themselves.

   Case Example: Stephanie sat in my office in disbelief and horror. She could not comprehend how someone could kill their own child. "Parenthood is the greatest gift and responsibility in the world. We should have some way of picking out people who are simply not cut out to raise kids."

   While Stephanie's distress is understandable, when we impose our own expectations on a reality that does not conform, we can feel very frustrated with ourselves or other people. Over time, this can diminish our sense of agency to help, as well as our overall satisfaction with our work. Difficulties accepting reality as it is and becoming stuck in "shoulds" contribute frequently to long-term psychological distress in the professionals I treat.

5. **Discounting the Positives**: Invalidating, reframing, or dismissing positive experiences, while paying more attention to negative experiences.

   Case Example: Jeff was distraught. He had been struggling with insomnia and hyperarousal symptoms, and today, an attending physician criticized him in front of a patient. He sat in my office feeling tremendous shame for struggling in his residency when his peers appeared to be coping just fine. "How is it that I haven't even finished my training and I am failing and falling apart already? Maybe I am just not cut out for medicine."

Focusing on negative experiences, particularly our shortcomings and mistakes, while minimizing our successes, can create a distorted perception of our skill and competence. Many highly skilled first responders and healthcare professionals have concluded that they are unsuited for the professions they have chosen, when this negative appraisal is simply not supported in reality.

Practice Exercise: Identifying Your Thinking Traps

Which of the thinking traps listed above do you engage in most often? Begin by noticing the specific self-talk as it occurs, label the specific thinking trap, and then notice the impact of thinking this way on how you feel and on your actions.

In the next chapter, we will learn and practice a commonly used technique to reframe unhelpful thinking patterns, the ABCD technique.

Key Points

What is one thing you are taking away from reading this chapter?

____

Action Plan

What is one way you can become more aware of habitual, unhelpful thinking patterns?

____

CHAPTER 15

Challenging Negative Automatic Thoughts

The first step in overcoming unhelpful thinking habits is to notice them when they occur and to recognize their impact on you. Becoming aware that a given thought process is unhelpful begins to create space between you and the belief or self-talk, starting an important process called cognitive defusion. Over time, you may notice that familiar thoughts have less of an impact on you emotionally and behaviorally. And with practice, you gradually develop the ability to change an unhelpful thought process to a healthier one. You become able to shift from unhelpful to more productive ways of making sense of situations—ways that serve you, your goals and your values. Practicing noticing, gaining distance from, and changing our ways of thinking enhances psychological flexibility, which is considered a cornerstone of mental health (see review by Kashdan and Rottenberg, 2010).

When practicing this skill, individuals are encouraged to ask themselves two questions about a given automatic thought. The inquiry is whether the thought or belief is *realistic,* reflective of the facts of the situation, and *helpful*, such that it aids in, rather than diminishes, our capacity to cope. The answer to whether a thought is helpful becomes apparent by the impact of the thought on the person— does it worsen or help manage painful situations? Does it motivate avoidance? Does it contribute to behavior that is aligned with your goals and values, or moves you further away from the life you want?

For first responders and healthcare providers, the inquiry, "Is this way of thinking *helpful*?" is often even more central than the question, "Is this way of thinking *realistic*?" This is because healthcare professionals and first responders frequently face objectively tragic, scary, and heartbreaking situations. Under these circumstances, it is understandable when distressing thoughts and feelings are provoked, such as worry or cynicism about people, and it may be easy to find evidence of this thinking in our experiences. Yet, healthcare professionals and first responders who wish to maintain psychological wellness should still try to practice arriving at ways of making sense of situations that are both realistic and do not contribute to hopelessness, despair, cynicism, or disillusionment.

While cognitive restructuring is very helpful, it is one of the most challenging psychological skills to master, as challenging our own automatic thoughts is not something we typically know how to do before engaging in therapy or reading a resource like this one. I encourage you to practice being both patient and persistent as you learn and master these strategies. Developing new, healthier thinking patterns can, in time, help you get through challenging situations with more ease and be less negatively impacted by the difficult events you encounter.

Challenging Unhelpful Thoughts Using the ABCD Technique

The first step in changing your thinking and response to stressful situations, discussed in the previous chapter, is to recognize the specific, unhelpful thoughts as they occur or immediately after. But what is to be done once we have identified the problematic thinking? This question is the focus of this section.

Challenging unhelpful thinking is simple but far from easy, and requires much practice. One common way to practice this skill is abbreviated using the acronym ABCD.

A (Activating Event): What was the event that triggered the unhelpful thought or belief?

B (Belief): What was the belief, cognition, or self-talk that came up?

C (Consequence): What emotions and behaviors did the thoughts above create?

D (Dispute): Is there another way to understand the situation, which is both realistic and helpful?

Use the ABCD method to identify some of your beliefs with regard to the situation that might be contributing to your suffering, and ask yourself, "Is this belief *realistic* and *helpful?*" If the answer is "no" to either of these, ask yourself the following questions to try and arrive at an alternate, more balanced appraisal.

1. Ask yourself: "What are the worst, the best, and the most realistic outcomes possible in this situation?"
2. Ask yourself: "Is there *any* evidence in the situation or in your history that contradicts this unhelpful belief?"
3. Ask yourself: "Is thinking this way allowing me to avoid some aspect of the situation, or a specific action or emotion?"
4. Ask yourself: "What experiences in my history may have conditioned me to think in this way?"
5. Ask yourself: "Is this way of thinking helping me cope or contributing to my suffering?"
6. Ask yourself: "What would I tell a close colleague or friend if they were in the same situation as me?"

CASE EXAMPLE | "I should have been able to save her"

Ali, a 50-year-old paramedic, recalled a call that occurred nearly two decades ago, but continued to impact him greatly. He was the first on the scene of a multi-car collision on an icy Canadian highway. As Ali shared, it was clear that this event was still very present and painful for him to revisit. In therapy, when describing this situation, he endorsed a mixture of sadness, intense guilt, and shame. He had attempted to resuscitate a young woman who succumbed to severe injuries. For two decades, he carried the belief that he "should have been able to save her."

When we examined this belief, we focused on the two probing questions described earlier: "Is this belief realistic given the facts of the situation?" and "Is this belief helpful or is it causing ongoing suffering?" With regard to the degree to which the belief reflected the facts or the reality of the situation, Ali recalled that the young woman's injuries were so extensive and severe that there is a near-zero likelihood that anyone would have been able to save her. He also acknowledged, in reference to the second question, that the belief that he could have (but failed to) save her had been a source of incredible pain and guilt for him ever since this call took place.

Over many sessions, Ali reflected on his belief and attempted to adopt a more realistic and helpful stance. He initially struggled to shift his feelings of guilt, even though he acknowledged that, analytically, he knew his belief was not realistic. This was frustrating and discouraging but Ali did not give up. Over many months, he practiced challenging his unhelpful thoughts, and began incorporatng mindfulness and self-compassion practices into his self-care routine. He first used these skills in other areas of his life that were less painful to think about, and he developed greater awareness of his thinking and greater psychological flexibility.

To demonstrate how ABCD can be practiced, consider what Ali's ABCD worksheet might look like:

A **(Activating event):** I was dispatched to a serious car accident. It was a mass casualty event, and I was assigned to care for a young woman who was in critical condition.

B **(Belief):** The woman I was caring for was still alive when I arrived and had I acted more quickly and decisively, I might have been able to save her. A better medic would have done a better job for her than I did. I failed her.

C **(Consequence):** I feel guilt and shame for not having done more for the young woman. Every time I respond to a serious MVA call or otherwise feel down on myself, this memory and intense guilt resurface, and it takes days before I am able to feel like myself again.

D **(Dispute):** I've gone over the memory hundreds of times in my mind. I keep getting the feeling that I should have done something to save her, but when I really look at it, I have no idea what it would have taken to save her. She was so young and still alive when we showed up on the scene. I remember how weak her pulse was and how much she had already bled. I moved as fast as I could. All of my colleagues say, "pal, you did what you could. Give yourself a break." Part of me knows that even the best medic in the world would not likely have saved her. I wish I could have done something, though. She had her whole life ahead of her and it was all gone in an instant. I now realize more and more that I was unlucky to have been dispatched to this call. I was young then too, and after this call, I was never the same.

As we revisited the memory of this call and tuned into his emotions, he noticed a gradual shift from predominant guilt to sadness and grief. He grieved for both the young woman and for his younger self, who was deeply impacted by this call. Gradually, the memory of this event became less distressing for him to discuss and remember, though it will always be a sad experience for him to recall from the early days of his career.

Practice Exercise

Recall a work-related situation that caused you some distress. Try to identify an unhelpful thought or belief that contributed to your distress. Use the prompts below to practice the ABCD skill.

A (Activating Event): Describe the situation that triggered this unhelpful thinking style:

____

B (Belief): Describe the thoughts and beliefs related to the situation:

____

C (Consequence): Describe the consequences of these thoughts and beliefs on your emotions and behavior:

____

D (Dispute): What is a realistic and helpful way to think of this situation?

____

Key Points

What is one thing you are taking away from reading this chapter?

____

Action Plan

What is one way you can begin to overcome the unhelpful thinking patterns that create suffering in your life?

____

CHAPTER 16

The Self-Critic: A Special Case of Unhelpful Thinking

We have seen how our thinking can be unhelpful or helpful depending on the way we make sense of events. Of all the unhelpful thinking patterns out there, self-criticism plays such a central role in the distress of many of my patients that I chose to give this issue some special attention. In my experience, the core of the suffering of many first responders and health-care professionals, regardless of the presenting symptoms, can be distilled to one central issue— the presence of negative core beliefs, often originating in early life. These negative core beliefs essentially become akin to sleeping porcupines in the psyche. They can lie dormant a great deal of the time, until they are triggered by painful life events, at which point they can become active, guide thinking and behavior, and cause tremendous pain.

Sooner or later, these sleeping psychic porcupines—the negative core beliefs we carry—are triggered by difficult situations such as facing uncertainty, criticism by others, or the experience of a negative patient outcome. When the negative core beliefs are awakened, we begin to engage in negative self-talk. This may take the form of doubting our actions, blaming ourselves for events, and generally berating ourselves internally. This pattern is often associated with intense anxiety, a tendency to experience shame, and we often cope through avoidance of any situation that has the potential to trigger these painful core beliefs in the future.

There are many ways that people develop negative core beliefs and a tendency toward self-doubt and self-criticism. The origins of this often date back to childhood experiences, but these can also arise later in life.

Here are a few common developmental scenarios that can lead to negative core beliefs and a tendency to be critical toward the self.

1. If you had an overly critical or demanding caregiver, one who'd use guilt or shame to shape your behavior, their statements may have become internalized and shaped negative core beliefs about yourself.

2. If you struggled in school (for example, due to undiagnosed ADHD or a learning disability) and received critical messages from teachers, peers, or caregivers that you are less capable or hardworking than others, as an adult, you might continue to believe yourself to be less smart or competent than others well into adulthood, even with plenty of evidence to the contrary.
3. If you were expected to behave more maturely than was appropriate for your age and development, such as being expected to provide extensive physical or emotional care to siblings or a parent, or contribute financially. You might have struggled to meet the unrealistic expectations placed on you and blamed yourself for this. This tendency for misplaced self-blame can become a lifelong habit.
4. If you experienced bullying or exclusion by peers, you may have come to believe that you are somehow lacking, inadequate, or unworthy of respect, love, or reciprocity.
5. If you experienced other forms of abuse or neglect by caregivers, witnessed domestic violence, or experienced parental separation or abandonment, you may have blamed yourself as a child. Children often conclude that there is something wrong with them that made them deserving of mistreatment or abandonment.

   Or you may have even been explicitly and unfairly blamed by others. This type of unjust criticism can form the basis of negative core beliefs about yourself, such as a belief you are unlovable or simply "bad."

While the histories described here are commonly found in individuals with a tendency toward self-criticism, it is not an absolute necessity for this tendency to stem from childhood adversity. For some individuals, a specific event or set of events, such as a critical work-related error, difficulties achieving a desired professional role, or being frequently criticized or abused in a relationship, can perpetuate negative beliefs about the self, a tendency toward self-criticism, and prominent feelings of shame.

To make matters more complex, self-criticism and shame tend to shape thinking and behavior in ways that maintain the negative beliefs and feelings, such as avoidance, perfectionism, and people-pleasing. Unfortunately, these behavioral adaptations not only fail to alleviate the underlying issues of self-criticism and shame, but also often do the opposite, reinforcing and strengthening negative core beliefs.

Negative beliefs about the self and the tendency toward self-criticism are among the trickiest, yet most common clinical issues to work on in therapy. One of the most rewarding experiences in my work has been witnessing patients gradually shift from self-criticism and self-loathing to self-compassion. When this shift begins to happen, the individual begins to increasingly show up as their whole, authentic self in both the therapy office and in their life. This blossoming is truly magnificent and is a privilege to witness and take part in.

Let us explore a few case examples of how negative beliefs about the self may originate in early life experiences, and how these are then maintained through thinking and behavior in adulthood.

1. **Case example**: Jordan, a police officer, grew up with a learning disability. Peers made fun of him for being slow to learn, and he came to believe that he was not as capable or bright as others.

   Distorted beliefs: In the police service, Jordan is often complimented by his sergeant for his work, but occasionally receives constructive feedback on his report writing, as do all newer officers. He often discounts the positive feedback and takes it for granted, but ruminates heavily on any criticism. Jordan remains convinced he is not as good of a cop as his peers and that he does not belong in the profession.

   Maintaining adult behavior: Jordan has always dreamed of joining the SWAT team at his police service, but he does not believe that he would ever be seen as worthy to even be considered. He has not taken the necessary steps to become eligible and has decided to stay on patrol duties even as he advances in his career and achieves the level of skill and experience needed to apply for the selective SWAT team.

2. **Case example:** Patrick is a general surgeon with a medical degree from a top medical school. He was raised by a cold, critical father, who had demanded that Patrick excel academically at all times. The only time he obtained his father's approval was when he brought home top grades and academic awards. Patrick learned to believe that his worth is measured by his career success, which led him to feel unworthy outside of his professional achievements. Patrick was not permitted to attend many social functions as he had to prioritize his studies, and thus missed out on many developmentally appropriate opportunities to form and maintain close friendships, and to experiment and gain confidence in dating.

Distorted beliefs: Now in his 40s, Patrick successfully secured a surgical position at a top hospital. His career is thriving, and several attractive women have expressed interest in dating him. While Patrick wishes to marry and have a family one day, he struggles to prioritize this over his career. He feels very anxious about dating, with a fear that when women get to know him beyond his career and financial standing, they will reject him as ugly, boring, and inexperienced in relationships and intimacy.

Maintaining adult behavior: Patrick avoids meeting women and becomes very anxious when he finds a woman attractive. When a coworker expresses interest in spending time together and getting to know each other, Patrick's anxiety kicks in. He uses his busy schedule as an excuse to avoid each opportunity.

3. **Case example:** Meghan was a highly compliant child in a large chaotic household, and was praised for being "good" – helpful, quiet, compliant, and not one to create trouble. Now, as a physician, she is well respected and liked by her peers but struggles to assert herself with peers and patients, and often feels secretly resentful for how she is treated.

   Distorted beliefs: Meghan is terrified of a patient filing a complaint, and she imagines that a complaint will result in her being fired. She goes above and beyond with patients, working through her meal breaks and staying late on shifts to make sure that her work is done exceptionally well. She is liked by peers and management, but is secretly resentful and depleted, and is not sure how long she will be able to tolerate this degree of exertion.

   Maintaining adult behavior: Meghan tolerates slights from patients without speaking assertively and does not challenge others on unreasonable requests. She worries frequently about making a mistake in her work, leading to self-doubt and excessive checking, and the prospect of making errors and being seen by her colleagues and superiors as incompetent creates considerable worry and anxiety in her day-to-day life.

These examples illustrate how negative self-relevant beliefs formed early in life can manifest in a first responder or healthcare professional's adult thinking and behavior. These behaviors maintain and reinforce the negative core beliefs making these patterns challenging to shift. Learning to recognize the possible origins of negative beliefs, recurrent self-critical self-talk, and behaviors that maintain these beliefs in the present makes it possible to slowly shift these sticky patterns, and doing this can have enormous psychological benefits.

How to Overcome a Tendency for Self-Criticism

If you carry negative core beliefs, they will often be triggered by current situations, and you will likely have a strong tendency to blame, criticize, and doubt yourself, as demonstrated in the examples offered earlier. I encourage you to commit to developing a more loving and compassionate relationship with yourself and realistic, helpful beliefs about yourself. This can be one of the most transformative changes anyone can make in the service of their mental health and life satisfaction. For first responders and healthcare professionals, this is especially key for emotional resilience in the face of the many occupational stressors you may face. I believe that each and every one of us (regardless of our profession or level of career success) carries some negative self-relevant beliefs that are not grounded in present reality, but rather are relics from our personal histories. It is only the frequency, potency, and impact of these limiting beliefs that vary from person to person.

Dr. Kristin Neff has researched and written extensively about self-compassion (which is covered in detail in Chapter 22). While many of us criticize ourselves in order to strive and improve our lives, this kind of attempt at inspiring change is often unhelpful. Dr. Kristin Neff asserts that it is actually self-compassion that nurtures resilience, emotional balance, and well-being, as well as motivation for growth. In contrast, self-criticism is implicated in anxiety and shame, emotional states that motivate avoidance and escape behaviors, not growth. Importantly, self-compassion research highlights the importance of knowing and accepting ourselves as we are, with our flaws, and realizing the shared humanity of being imperfect. We all have areas of struggle, and we don't have to be perfect to love, care for, and support ourselves as we navigate the challenges of life (Neff, 2015; Neff & Germer, 2017). My clinical experience fully supports these conclusions. In my work, I find time and time again that it is self-compassion, and not self-criticism, which facilitates the motivation to learn, strive, and take steps outside our comfort zones, allowing us to grow and achieve our goals.

The following are some recommendations and strategies to help overcome negative self-judgments and self-criticism. It is important to note, however, that transforming self-criticism into self-compassion is often a very challenging change that takes time and may require the help of a skilled clinician. Understanding the cost of negative self-talk and setting the intention to become more self-compassionate is an important first step on the journey to overcoming this set of challenges. I offer here a few suggestions for how to begin to shift away from self-criticism and begin to shift underlying negative beliefs. Note that practicing these strategies for self-criticism combined with the complementary strategies to enhance self-compassion (Chapter 22) may accelerate the change from negative self-talk to a more supportive, compassionate relationship with the self.

1. **Name your self-critical voice.** Giving your inner critical voice a funny name can be very helpful. This might sound strange or silly at first, but this accomplishes two things. First, the aim is to reduce our complete identification with the self-critical, repetitive, conditioned messages the self-condemning voice produces. Giving it a name highlights that it is a separate entity and not you. Second, giving the self-critic a silly name makes the experience of acknowledging it a little lighter emotionally, perhaps even slightly amusing, which can change the emotional tone of engaging with this painful content. When you notice the self-critical part of you arise, first acknowledge it. This may be a simple, "Hello Critical Carl – I see that you're back." Begin to ask yourself, "Is there any other way to make sense of this situation?" and "What would I say to a friend if this were happening to them and not to me?" The ABCD framework discussed earlier can be very useful for this purpose. Be patient with yourself; this type of change takes time.
2. **Reflect on what the self-criticism may have protected you from in the past, and what it may be trying to protect you from today.** According to Dr. Richard Schwartz, creator of a rapidly growing treatment modality called Internal Family Systems (IFS), "there are no bad parts," which includes the parts of us that generate self-criticism and associated emotions and behaviors. All of our parts, including the self-critical ones, are trying to be helpful to us. It is our job to figure out why a part may be protecting us in this specific way, and why this tendency and underlying negative core beliefs came about (Schwartz, 2021).
3. **Act as if you were not self-critical.** As demonstrated in the examples above, negative beliefs about the self and self-criticism often contribute to avoidance, which protects us from failure in the short term but reinforces our sense of inadequacy and unworthiness in the longer term. The good news is that it is often easier to shift behavior than

to change beliefs. For example, if Jordan or Patrick from the case examples above were my patients, I'd encourage them to take small risks in doing things that could prove very beneficial for their overall well-being. These recommendations could be encouraging Jordan to apply for the SWAT team, or for Patrick to accept a colleague's invitation to go for coffee, even if they have anxiety and urges to avoid these situations. Often, our negative beliefs are not grounded in reality and the negative predictions we make do not actually materialize. By taking small, consistent steps to push past our fears, we can begin to gather real-life evidence that we are capable, likable, and worthy of what we wish for. The CBT skill of Behavioral Experiments (Chapter 17) is a structured way to do just this.

4. **Recognize the costs of your self-criticism for both you and those around you.** Reflect often on the ways negative core beliefs and self-criticism may be limiting you professionally and personally. When you are able to recognize the negative consequences of negative self-talk, it may increase motivation to overcome this pattern, either on your own or with the help of a therapist.
5. **Recognize that frequent self-criticism is, more often than not, a response to adversity and trauma.** While not all highly self-critical people had abuse or neglect in their histories, for many, these beliefs arose as a result of adversity, unmet needs, or facing demands that were beyond their capabilities at the time. This is common. The more compassion and understanding we can generate toward ourselves for whatever forms of adversity we may have experienced, the more likely we are to extend compassion and grace toward ourselves in the present.
6. **Recognize that frequent self-criticism is incompatible with well-being.** Given the negative emotional, behavioral, and even physical health consequences of chronic self-criticism, this pervasive habit is not compatible with a mentally and physically healthy life, nor with thriving in a healthcare or first responder job with its inherent multitude of stressors. If your goal is to maintain your health and a positive outlook while working in one of these challenging roles, it is essential to overcome negative self-relevant beliefs and chronic, harsh self-criticism and develop a more positive, supportive relationship with your self. This does not mean you do not acknowledge limitations, errors, or knowledge gaps and work on them. It simply means

you refrain from blaming and beating yourself up in situations where this is not warranted.

7. **Be patient and persistent with change.** Overcoming a tendency toward self-critical self-talk takes time. Begin to incorporate the practices in this book (such as mindfulness, self-compassion practices, and reframing negative automatic thoughts), and be patient with yourself if it takes time to see the desired change. If you struggle to see a difference in your thought patterns when working on these issues alone, the support of an experienced therapist may be helpful in significantly diminishing self-criticism and becoming more supportive and compassionate toward yourself.

Reflection

- Can you identify the unhelpful thinking styles and behaviors that are impacting each individual described earlier in this section?
- If you had an opportunity to speak to each of these individuals, what would you say or recommend to each person to help shift their unhelpful beliefs and the associated behaviors?
- What is the role that negative beliefs and the tendency for self-criticism have in your own current difficulties?
- In what types of situations are you most vulnerable to self-critical self-talk?

Key Points

What is one thing you are taking away from reading this chapter?

___

Action Plan

What is one way you can begin to overcome negative beliefs about yourself and habitual self-criticism?

___

CHAPTER 17

Understanding and Overcoming Avoidance

Avoidance in the context of mental health refers to the deliberate effort to prevent, escape, or minimize exposure to thoughts, feelings, situations, or experiences that are distressing or threatening. Avoidance is considered to play a central role in maintaining mental health challenges. On one level, avoidance makes complete sense; it is entirely natural to want to escape from stimuli that cause us distress. However, when avoidance becomes habitual, it can directly contribute to mental health difficulties. It is no surprise, then, that in many therapy modalities, there is an emphasis on identifying or overcoming patterns of avoidance. We will devote some time in this section to understanding avoidance and its various manifestations, as well as considering interventions to overcome avoidance, in order to reduce its negative long-term consequences.

There are three broad types of avoidance, including:

1. ***Behavioral Avoidance***: Avoiding specific situations or actions. *Example*: Someone with social anxiety may avoid parties or public speaking.
2. ***Cognitive Avoidance***: Pushing away or suppressing distressing thoughts. *Example*: Avoiding thinking about a traumatic event because the memory causes painful emotions to arise.
3. ***Emotional Avoidance:*** Trying to avoid feeling certain emotions through distraction, denial, or numbing. *Example*: Using alcohol or drugs to suppress sadness or fear.

Why Do We Avoid?

Avoidance is typically a coping strategy, or a way to manage strong emotions, such as anxiety or shame. It often provides short-term relief by reducing discomfort in the moment – we simply do not do (or think about, or feel) that which causes fear or distress. However, avoidance can make symptoms worse over the long term. Avoidance is often seen as a causal and maintaining factor in mental health difficulties, and avoidance tends to make us feel stuck or limited in growth and pursuing our life goals.

In healthcare professionals and first responders, avoidance can take many forms. Police officers and paramedics with PTSD, for example, tend to avoid places, people, and objects that remind them of particularly traumatic emergency calls. Many of my patients across vocations refrain from talking about perceived errors or their own shortcomings due to feelings of shame. And many of us use emotional avoidance strategies such as keeping very busy with work, excessive online shopping, emotional eating, or substance abuse for the purposes of subduing negative emotional states. These attempts at coping maintain or worsen psychological difficulties. Here are some ways that avoidance can contribute to and exacerbate our psychological challenges:

- **Avoidance reinforces anxiety and fear**. Individuals who rely on avoidance never learn that they can handle the situations or things they avoid, a strategy which perpetuates anxiety (e.g., if I avoid speaking up in meetings because I believe I would not be articulate enough, I deprive myself of the opportunity to experience successful participation).
- **Avoidance limits functioning by interfering with work, relationships, education, and self-care.** Avoidance resulting from self-doubt or self-criticism prevents us from taking the necessary steps to progress or grow, which can lead to missed opportunities (e.g., avoiding job applications and interviews poses difficulties for career advancement).
- **Avoidance increases stress, as situations that are avoided often compound due to inaction.** For instance, if I avoid the medical investigation recommended to me, fail to pay bills when they are due, or avoid having a tough conversation that is needed, the underlying situation does not go away. In fact, it often worsens (e.g, a medical condition advances without treatment) or becomes even more difficult to resolve when eventually confronted.
- **Avoidance often leads to withdrawal from meaningful activities and relationships.** When we avoid difficult conversations in relationships, a distance can grow as unspoken feelings and resentments are permitted to accumulate. In this way, avoidance makes it more difficult

to maintain existing relationships and create meaningful new ones. Compassionately confronting, rather than avoiding, difficult conversations can lead to increased intimacy and trust. It provides opportunities for us and those we are close to compromise, problem-solve areas of challenge, and find ways to meet the needs of both participants.

CASE EXAMPLE | "What I don't know can't hurt me"

Lise was a retired nurse in her early 60s who had previously worked for many years in an oncology unit of a large urban hospital, where she cared for many women battling breast cancer. While many of her patients made a full recovery, some did not. Some young, vibrant women deteriorated quickly and died within a matter of months as a result of this disease. Now a postmenopausal woman with a family history of cancer, Lise has been too afraid to undergo routine mammograms to ensure that she herself does not have breast cancer. Her primary health physician has brought this up several times and eventually gave up trying to persuade her to go. For Lise, the thought of going for a mammogram and being told she has advanced cancer terrifies her. She has booked and canceled mammograms a handful of times, and has since given up, which only compounds her fear of going for the first time. She justifies her avoidance of this testing with the belief that if she is intended to die from breast cancer, "so be it."

This example illustrates how avoidance can become problematic by interfering with important, value-congruent steps we need to take. Avoidance is very common, and identifying and gradually overcoming avoidance is a major part of therapy across a variety of difficulties, especially anxiety and traumatic stress. One of the most commonly used and most effective CBT tools for overcoming patterns of avoidance is the Behavioral Experiment, which is described below.

Practice Exercise: The Behavioral Experiment

Designing a CBT Behavioral Experiment involves identifying, testing and revising unhelpful beliefs that maintain avoidance. In other words, it requires engaging in real-world activities that we may be avoiding because we hold very negative beliefs about what might happen if we participate. The aim is to gather evidence that challenges distorted, unrealistic thinking. Here are a few guiding prompts to help structure such experiments:

1. Identify a situation to confront
What situation will provide an opportunity to test out your belief? When and where will you carry this out?

2. Make predictions
Be specific—what do you expect will happen if you engage rather than avoid this situation?

3. Conduct the experiment
Note any observations and how you felt before, during, and immediately after the experiment

4. Reflect on the outcome and draw conclusions
What did you learn from this experiment, and how will you use this information in the future?

CASE EXAMPLE | Rediscovering Her Voice

Louisa, a physician in her mid-40s, described her struggle with assertive communication at the workplace. She struggled to set boundaries with talkative and demanding patients, and as a result, her appointments frequently ran over time. Additionally, she often felt dismissed by the clinic manager and pressured to take on new patients when she did not feel she had the space in her caseload to do so. She shared that seeing too many patients in a day, as well as having appointments go over the alotted time, both led to feelings of exhaustion, resentment and overwhelm. This was beginning to impact her family negatively as she often stayed late to finish her documentation and came home exhausted and depleted. In therapy, she set goals to become more direct with patients to keep to the alotted appointment time and to decline new referrals when she felt overscheduled.

Below is an example of how the CBT skill of Behavioral Experiment was used by Louisa to overcome avoidance and become more assertive at her workplace.

1. Identify a situation to confront

Louisa's example: I would like to practice setting boundaries with my patients. I will practice being more directive with patients and end appointments that run more than 5 minutes over the designated time.

2. Make predictions

Louisa's example: I worry that patients will become upset or angry when I enforce the time limit and ask them to save issues for another appointment. I am fearful that some patients might complain to the clinic manager.

3. Conduct the Experiment and record observations

Louisa's example: Of my twenty patients this week, I had to set limits on time with eight patients. Most were respectful of the time limit, and two expressed some frustration at not having an opportunity to discuss all of their concerns. So far, I don't think anyone has complained to the clinic manager.

4. Reflect on the outcome and draw conclusions

Louisa's example: While patients do not necessarily like being limited on time this way, they are generally receptive to the change. It has made my workdays feel more manageable and I feel less stressed as I am no longer constantly behind schedule. I am also no longer working overtime on most days. I believe I need to continue setting these boundaries with my patients for my own well-being.

Practice Exercise: Overcoming Avoidance

Let's practice designing a Behavioral Experiment to help you overcome avoidance in a situation that is difficult for you to tackle. Please pick a situation in your life where you typically engage in avoidance but would like to be able to confront, being as specific as possible. Try to find a situation that will allow you to complete the experiment several times, to determine what tends to happen when you approach instead of avoid.

The avoided situation I will confront is as follows:

____

I predict that if I overcome my avoidance, the following will happen:

____

The experiment I will conduct in order to test out my prediction is as follows (be as specific and detailed as possible!):

____

Here is what I have learned from conducting this experiment:

____

Key Points

What is one thing you are taking away from reading this chapter?

____

Action Plan

What is one way you can overcome problematic avoidance in your life?

____

SECTION 3: CARING FOR YOUR EMOTIONS

CHAPTER 18

Who Needs Emotions Anyway?

Human beings have evolved both analytical and emotional responses to deal with stressful events. Of these, the emotional side of things is often harder to make sense of and deal with because emotional experiences can be intense, confusing, and lack the clarity of thinking. For many, thinking can also serve as a way to keep a distance from feelings.

First responders and healthcare professionals, in my experience, tend to rely especially heavily on their thinking and problem-solving skills. For these folks, learning to recognize, tolerate, and care for themselves emotionally tends to be quite new and challenging. I believe that this is partially due to the demands of healthcare and first responder roles, and also due to most of us not having had formal training or modeling by caregivers on how to cope with and process intense emotions in healthy ways. The habit of using thinking to analyze one's way out of stress and treating emotions as pesky distractions is common in dealing with adversity, but it is not an effective way to cope with distress.

I would like to use this opportunity to share some strategies to help you become more comfortable with identifying, tolerating, making sense of, and fully processing your negative emotions.

The DBT (Dialectical Behavior Therapy) treatment approach focuses on integrating the wisdom of the mind and the wisdom of the heart (i.e., emotions). DBT is based on the premise that emotions are helpful and necessary because they serve several functions. Specifically, emotions motivate us to act, convey important information to others, and convey important information to ourselves. Understanding these critical functions helps individuals to both understand and regulate their emotions more effectively.

1. **Communication with others:** Emotions are a powerful way to communicate our needs and desires to others, both verbally and

nonverbally. For example, we may find ourselves becoming tearful when we are in emotional pain or have recently experienced loss. Seeing our sadness and tears, those around us may be moved to offer help or comfort through words or affection.

2. **Communication with ourselves**: Emotions provide valuable information about our own internal state and the situation we are in, as described earlier in this book. Our emotions represent a different, yet equally valuable, source of information about the world compared to our minds. There is a reason the term "gut instinct" is used to describe awareness that differs from cognitive processes. Many patients describe feeling appropriate and valid anger arising in the body when they are verbally disrespected by a patient or a colleague. In both of these cases, your body is using its affective system to let you know that "something isn't right" in the situation, and this emotional and physical change mobilizes you to take effective action to correct it.
3. **Motivation for action**: Emotions prepare us for action, urging us to behave in certain ways based on our emotional state. Specific emotions typically arise in particular situations and motivate predictable reactions. For example, anger might prompt us to defend ourselves, while fear might motivate us to escape a dangerous situation.

To become more skilled at processing your emotions, a useful first step is to practice being curious about what a given emotion is trying to tell you and those around you. If this reminds you of the discussion of mindfulness (Chapter 6), you are exactly right. The first step in knowing how to respond to a strong emotion is recognizing the emotion and its triggers accurately and non-judgmentally. This is yet another way in which mindfulness of something (in this case, emotion) is a necessary precursor to skillful coping with the situation.

The following chapters will focus on specific emotions that often arise for first responders and healthcare professionals in the context of their work, how these emotions can create difficulties, and strategies for processing them and overcoming the associated difficulties.

CHAPTER 19

Understanding Anger

Anger, like any other emotion, is a universal and necessary human emotion with important, adaptive, and necessary functions that help keep us safe. In other words, anger plays a crucial role in enabling us to survive and thrive in our relations with others and in the general challenges we face in life. Anger is the emotion we naturally feel when we are thwarted from achieving a goal or taking an action that is important to us, when our needs are unseen and unmet by others, and when our boundaries (physical or psychological) are violated.

Anger also informs us that something is not sitting well, or that an event or action is misaligned with values important to us. Anger is adaptive in that it mobilizes us to defend ourselves against threats or injustice, giving us the affective energy to set boundaries, pursue important goals despite obstacles, and communicate to those around us that we need something to change. However, despite it being a helpful and necessary emotion, many people I have spoken to have significant struggles with anger. Interestingly, the difficulties usually take one of two extreme forms - individuals report that they either access anger excessively, when other emotions may be more appropriate, or they have difficulties accessing anger at all, even when it is absolutely appropriate.

When There Is Not Enough Anger

It is important that we can access our anger without avoiding or suppressing it. Anger provides us with a means to set limits, can indicate self-worth, and acts as a barometer of our value systems. Patients who struggle with accessing their anger often report struggling with self-doubt, low self-esteem and self-criticism, and engage in adaptations including people-pleasing, lack of assertiveness and boundaries, and over-exertion, leading to depletion of their emotional resources and resilience. They are often frustrated and dissatisfied, both at the workplace and in personal relationships. In my experience, the histories of many patients who struggle this way involve a caregiver, typically a parent, who tended to display dysregulated anger - perhaps a mother or father who shouted, cursed, name-called, or even showed physical aggression when angry, and often another caregiver who accommodated to the will of the more forceful person. From witnessing this dynamic, it is easy to believe that anger can only be expressed through aggression or suppressed entirely. As adults, these individuals often fear their anger and develop mechanisms to suppress it. Over time, not only does the anger not express itself externally, but individuals struggle to feel and experience this important emotion internally, even when it is completely appropriate.

With patients who have this difficulty, therapy often involves regaining access to adaptive anger and becoming more skillful in expressing it assertively. Patients are often relieved to know that, aside from erupting in rage and suppressing anger, there are, in fact, a variety of assertive options for expressing anger without necessarily harming relationships. In fact, authentic expressions of needs and boundaries, which are often facilitated by appropriate anger, can strengthen healthy, reciprocal relationships. Aside from practicing awareness of anger arising through mindfulness (see Chapter 6), the DBT skill of DEAR MAN, described later in this chapter, provides a useful framework for practicing assertive expression of needs and boundaries.

When There Is Too Much Anger

On the other end of the spectrum, some individuals seek help because they are easily triggered to feel angry, even when the trigger does not seem to warrant the intensity of their emotional reaction. Such individuals often also have difficulties in accessing other emotions, such as fear and sadness.

In my experience, this type of difficulty is more common in occupations such as law enforcement, firefighting, surgical specialties in medicine, and the military. Anecdotally, I have heard from patients that it is more acceptable to express feelings of being "pissed off" and to release emotional steam using colorful language choices, whereas genuine expressions of fear or sadness incur social judgment for not being "tough" or "masculine." Thus, individuals essentially learn to convert the sadness or fear into anger, allowing the emotional energy to be expressed in an altered form. However, the underlying emotions remain unacknowledged and unexpressed, which can lead to prolonged psychological distress. The case example of Mila, a police officer (Chapter 21), illustrates this. This pattern is often causal to the development of traumatic stress symptoms, and so much of the work in therapy is related to gaining access to the primary emotions underlying the anger. The Anger Iceberg (Figure 3) provides a visual illustration for the process by which the emotion of anger often conceals more vulnerable emotions, including sadness, hurt, fear, and many others.

To understand how this works, let us consider an example. Imagine that today is your birthday. It is already mid-afternoon and your romantic partner has not acknowledged the special day, and in fact, appears to have totally forgotten. Take a moment to reflect on what emotion or emotions this may trigger in you. For many, primary emotions of sadness, disappointment, and hurt at not being acknowledged or celebrated may arise. Now imagine what you might actually say to your partner. For many of us, instead of expressing our sadness and hurt directly, we might feel safer saying something sarcastic, labeling our partner as an uncaring or "bad" person, or acting cold, unaffectionate and distant. Most of these behaviors and statements stem from anger, rather than the underlying hurt or sadness.

This switch from sadness to anger may seem simple, but this longstanding adaptation of covering sadness with anger is a central factor in psychological distress and dysfunction, in my experience. This is because, in any event, when underlying emotions are not acknowledged or expressed, genuine healing cannot occur effectively. These unexpressed emotions remain in the body waiting to be acknowledged and processed. This is why we therapists emphasize, in a safe space such as the therapy office, that patients practice coming into contact with the underlying (also called primary) emotions. Moving from the suppression of emotion to its expression is a common shift that occurs in the process of trauma-focused psychotherapy and is a sign of progress and healing. Not only does this reduce the likelihood of lingering psychological distress, but it usually improves dynamics within close relationships. It is far easier to be understood and elicit the support we need from others when our emotions are clearly expressed than when they are misleading. Imagine how much more effective it would be to tell your partner, "I am really hurt and disappointed that you forgot my birthday," as opposed to conveying this with passive aggression or emotional withdrawal.

Other patients have a different challenge. They have a critical and judgmental style of relating to others, so pervasive that it seems to be a part of their personality. Unlike those who become irritable as a result of discrete traumatic experiences, the latter group appears to be characterologically critical, prone to anger, and struggles to relate to and empathize with others, a deficit that remains fairly consistent throughout their lives. In my experience, this, too, is often an early-life adaptation to adversity, such as being subjected to judgment and frequent criticism by parents. For individuals who struggle this way, the clinical approach I take is quite similar to the one taken for more discrete trauma, including processing of any traumatic experiences and fostering increased awareness, identification, and tolerance of emotions aside from anger. In this case, the underlying emotions, often grief and shame, may be more challenging and take longer to access, and the overall patterns may be more challenging to change significantly.

For most who struggle with becoming angry too easily, much of the work in therapy tends to focus on gradually promoting access to the underlying emotions and their healthy expression. As the underlying emotions are accessed and tolerated, the more generalized, pervasive anger can begin to subside. Even after this process, patients naturally still experience anger from time to time, but it is more time-bound and specific to situations where anger makes sense. Specific bouts of adaptive anger can be used to inform wise action but anger does not linger as a chronic background hum any longer.

In addition to accessing the emotions underlying anger, patients who struggle with being anger-prone often also benefit from training and practice in mindfully tolerating anger without immediately reacting. Using the STOP mindfulness practice outlined in DBT (Chapter 6) when one feels upset and angry can help patients begin to treat their anger as a source of potentially useful information. This check-in and delay in reacting also allows patients to implement other skills such as the ABCD framework to challenge the judgments and assumptions underlying the anger (Chapter 15) and radical acceptance (Chapter 23) of the upsetting actions of other people. Tolerating anger is much more challenging than immediately reacting to it, but this shift can often be immensely protective to close relationships which are often taxed by an individual's tendency for reactivity when anger arises.

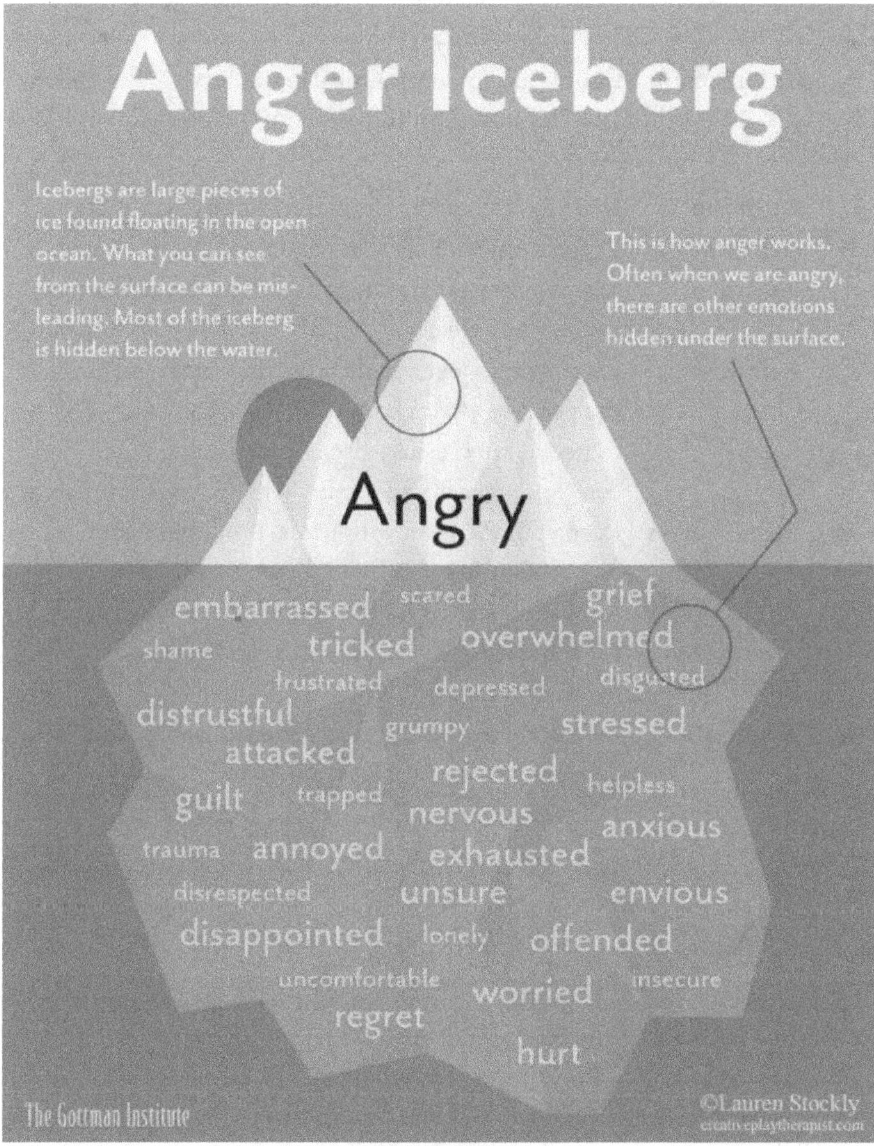

Figure 3. The Anger Iceberg (Stockley, 2022). Reprinted with permission.

Practice Exercise: DEAR MAN

A useful acronym to guide us in communicating assertively is DEAR MAN, a DBT skill that promotes mindful communication of needs, wishes, and boundaries.

D	**Describe**	Describe the current situation. Stick to the facts.
E	**Express**	Express your feelings and opinions about the situation.
A	**Assert**	Assert yourself by asking for what you need and saying "no" clearly.
R	**Reinforce**	Reinforce the person ahead of time by explaining the positive effects of getting what you want or need. If necessary, also clarify the negative consequences of not getting what you want or need.
M	**Mindfulness**	Keep your focus on your goals. Don't get distracted or go off topic.
A	**Appear Confident**	Appear effective and competent. Use a confident tone of voice, physical manner, and good eye contact.
N	**Negotiate**	Be willing to give to get. Offer and ask for other solutions to the problem. Focus on what will work.

Figure 4. DBT Interpersonal Effectiveness skill DEAR MAN (Linehan, 2015). Reprinted with permission.

CASE EXAMPLE | Rediscovering Her Voice (continued)

In Chapter 17, we met Louisa, a physician who was struggling to be assertive with her clinic manager about not having space to accommodate new patients. We learned that Louisa was overworking and beginning to experience burnout, and Louisa practiced the CBT skill of the Behavioral Experiment to begin setting boundaries with patients regarding appointment lengths. Let us see how Louisa might use the DEAR MAN framework to discuss her concerns about her caseload with her manager.

D - Describe: Describe the current situation. Stick to the facts.
Louisa's example: "I have taken on several new patients in the past sixty days, and I am struggling to find time to see all of my existing patients

during my clinic hours. I am finding that I have to stay 1 to 2 hours past my shift to finish my documentation almost every day."

E - Express: Express your feelings and opinions about the situation.
Louisa's example: "I'm finding my current caseload difficult to manage, and I worry about taking on additional patients this month. Coming home late every evening is creating stress and starting to take a toll on my family, as well."

A - Assert: Assert yourself by asking for what you need and saying "no" clearly.
Louisa's example: "I'd like to hold off on taking new patients for at least two to three months, to be able to provide high-quality care to my existing patients without further adding to my family stress and burnout. When I feel that my caseload is manageable again, I will accept new referrals."

R - Reinforce: Reinforce the person ahead of time by explaining the positive effects of getting what you want or need. If necessary, also clarify the negative consequences of not getting what you want or need.
Louisa's example: "I'd like to continue to provide high-quality care to our clinic's patients and give each one the time they require to maintain our practice's excellent reputation. Taking on any new referrals will make it difficult to continue to do so."

M - Mindfulness: Keep your focus on your goals. Don't get distracted or go off topic.
Louisa's example: Louisa had a number of other concerns to raise with the clinic manager, but she chose to leave them for another day and focus this discussion solely on her caseload.

A - Appear Confident: Appear effective and competent. Use a confident tone of voice, physical manner, and good eye contact.
Louisa's example: Louisa felt nervous about being this direct with the clinic manager, but she practiced role-playing this with her therapist and with a trusted colleague. She was deliberate in speaking clearly, with an appropriate tone and volume, and maintaining eye contact despite her anxiety.

N - Negotiate: Be willing to give to get. Offer and ask for other solutions to the problem. Focus on what will work.
Louisa's example: Louisa shared with her manager that she was prepared to take on additional referrals later in the year, as she was confident that by then her existing caseload would require less of her time.

Practice Exercise: DEAR MAN

Now it is your turn. If there is a conversation you would like to have, but have been avoiding for some time, consider how you would frame your delivery using the DEAR MAN framework. The prompts are provided for your reference.

D - Describe: Describe the current situation. Stick to the facts.

____

E - Express: Express your feelings and opinions about the situation.

____

A - Assert: Assert yourself by asking for what you need and saying "no" clearly.

____

R - Reinforce: Reinforce the person in advance by explaining the positive effects of getting what you want or need. If necessary, also clarify the negative consequences of not getting what you want or need.

____

Consider how you will implement the additional communication principles below:

M - Mindfulness: Keep your focus on your goals. Don't get distracted or go off topic.

____

A- Appear Confident: Appear effective and competent. Use a confident tone of voice, physical manner, and good eye contact.

____

N- Negotiate: Be willing to give to get. Offer and ask for other solutions to the problem. Focus on what will work.

____

Recommendations for difficulties with anger

- **Begin noticing your anger non-judgmentally**. Practice noticing anger and how it manifests in the body, as well as the thoughts that accompany it. Each time you notice anger arising, practice noting how intense the anger feels in this moment, using a scale from 0 (very mild) to 10 (extremely intense). Try to catch anger soon after it arises, when it is still mild, and notice how that feels.
- **Inquire whether your anger is alerting you to a need that has not been met or a boundary that may need to be set.** Anger is like a protective friend you carry within, one who is trying to alert you to what is important to you. Try to be curious and receptive to the message carried within the emotion. You might even try asking your anger directly: what feels unsafe or unjust in this moment? What action do you need me to take, and what do you need me to say to make the situation feel less unsafe or unjust?
- **Notice that you can experience and tolerate intense anger without acting on it.** Rageful behavior is not an inevitable consequence of anger, unlike what many people have learned to believe. It is possible, especially with practice, to take time to regulate, reflect, and choose the best course of action before taking the next steps, even when feeling intense anger.
- **Investigate whether anger is the primary emotion, or whether it may be covering more vulnerable emotions.** Use the Anger Iceberg diagram (Figure 3) to notice what other emotions may be present, alongside the anger. If you identify another emotion, ask yourself, "What is this emotion telling me about this situation?" This can begin to shift attention from anger to the underlying (primary) emotion.

- **Notice and anticipate your triggers**. Prepare for or avoid triggering situations whenever possible. Notice which situations and people leave you most vulnerable to anger. Ahead of engaging in triggering situations, consider how you will cope if strong anger arises. Which skills might you use? Consider using DEAR MAN to clearly articulate your needs and boundaries, or consider removing yourself from the situation if assertiveness is unlikely to be effective.
- **Consider making changes.** If you find yourself triggered by the same situations and people in your life again and again, and your efforts at assertiveness and boundary-setting do not yield change in these relational patterns, consider whether it may be possible to lessen your exposure or the impact of these situations on you in the long term. Prioritize your physical and emotional well-being whenever possible in making such decisions.

Reflection

- How would you describe your difficulties with anger?
- What people, places, and situations make you most vulnerable to experience difficulties with anger?
- How would you like to improve your coping with anger?
- What strategies have you tried so far to manage your difficulties with anger? What was helpful and what was not?

Key Points

What is one thing you are taking away from reading this chapter?

____

Action Plan

What is one action you can take to improve your coping with anger?

____

CHAPTER 20

Understanding Guilt and Shame

This chapter will be devoted to two closely related, yet distinct, emotions: guilt and shame. Working to overcome feelings of guilt and shame is a common focus in therapy in the treatment of first responders and healthcare professionals. Let us first define guilt and shame, and explore how these emotions commonly impact individuals working in healthcare and first responder roles.

Guilt

Guilt is the "feeling bad" that we experience due to having taken what we perceive to be wrong action or actions (including failure to do what we perceive as the "right thing"). Guilt is adaptive because it prompts us to take responsibility, attempt to repair relationships, and it also alerts us to a violation of personal ethics and values. In its positive form, what we can call justified guilt — guilt that represents remorse for a true violation —can lead to action to repair a relationship. This strengthens trust and intimacy by signaling to others that you care about the impact of your actions.

Justified guilt can be a very helpful emotion and has an important role in keeping us aligned with our own ethics and values. Think of guilt as our internal alarm system, triggered when we violate our inner values giving rise to an unpleasant emotional state that prompts us to take corrective action. For example, Imagine that, due to being especially fatigued or stressed, your partner at work is curt and critical about your handling of a given emergency call, leading to hurt and anger within you. If you express this to them, it would actually be very helpful for your partner to experience some measure of guilt about talking to you in an insensitive, harshly critical way. Guilt may lead him to take responsibility for hurting you, and he may apologize, which could lead to increased trust and a deepening of your professional relationship.

On the other hand, guilt can arise when it is not justified, in that it does not relate to an actual violation of your values or ethics or to anything you did that was wrong. Unjustified guilt, however, tells you that you did something wrong when this is not actually the case. Take the previously introduced case example of Ali, a paramedic who struggled to accept the death of a victim in a motor vehicle collision (Chapter 15), whose life he attempted but was ultimately unable to save. Ali carried the guilt of not having saved the young woman for two decades. Ali's guilt was perhaps understandable, but it was unjustified, as he had not done anything wrong — in fact, he had done everything in his power to save the young woman. Unjustified guilt is extra painful and tough to overcome because there is usually no apology to offer and no corrective action available to make amends or correct the situation.

Ali's example is not based on a single patient I have had, but rather, on the dozens of first responders and healthcare professionals I have treated who have carried the heavy load of intense, unjustified guilt. Often these individuals were faced with tragic situations and had little actual control over the outcome. They typically do everything they can, but when their efforts to help do not yield the desired outcome, they develop feelings of personal responsibility for the tragedy. They commonly endorse beliefs in the form, "If only I had .. the person would have survived." In my experience, this is one of the most common ways individuals become psychologically injured by a traumatic event. The guilt can be a heavy burden carried for a long time, even for the remainder of the individual's life, and can have many painful consequences.

Shame

Shame is the emotion we feel when we perceive ourselves globally as flawed, inadequate, as well as bad in the eyes of others, or in our own eyes. Unlike guilt, which is focused on specific actions and choices, shame is a more holistic, negative evaluation of the self. Guilt is painful, but because of its holistic and negative impact on how we see ourselves (or how we believe others see us), shame is often even more intensely painful, an almost intolerable emotion.

As with guilt, a distinction can be made between justified shame and unjustified shame. Justified shame would be appropriate when someone has acted in a way or engaged in behaviors that they, or others, would find reprehensible, such as engaging in fraud or child abuse. When our behavior genuinely violates deeply held values or social expectations, shame can help bring insight, motivate us to course-correct, and prompt us to attempt to repair relationships

Unlike guilt, I find that the shame that I witness in many patients while in therapy is almost exclusively unjustified, excessive, and maladaptive, often with origins in early trauma and adversity. Shame creates enormous suffering for individuals and motivates avoidance and escape behaviors meant to reduce this experience. Tragically, shame motivates behaviors such as self-isolation, self-neglect, self-soothing attempts using addictive behaviors, and self-punishment. The triad of trauma, self-criticism and maladaptive shame is a common set of challenges that puts individuals, including first responders and healthcare professionals, at great emotional and physiological risks. Overcoming this triad is often a focus of psychotherapy for many people.

The good news is that it is possible to overcome difficulties with guilt and shame. This is at the core of what I help people to do daily and it is a meaningful, inspiring, and challenging part of mental health work. The strategies outlined throughout this book, most especially mindfulness, self-compassion, and changing self-critical beliefs can help reduce shame over time. This is often done alongside the processing of the traumatic and difficult experiences that gave rise to the unjustified shame in the first place. If you struggle with feelings of shame, working to overcome them, ideally with the support of an experienced mental health clinician, can make a tremendous difference in your life.

Guilt and Shame Proneness

Difficulties with excessive guilt and shame for many of my patients began early in life, long before they became first responders or healthcare providers. In my experience, the following types of family-of-origin dynamics are common in the personal histories of individuals who struggle with guilt or shame as adults:

1. **Being expected to follow strict cultural, familial, or religious rules with little space for individual expression and choice.**
   In situations where compliance with strict familial, religious, or cultural rules is expected, failure to conform is often met with anger and pressure to conform. These reactions elicit guilt and shame. An individual growing up in such an environment may begin to associate any expression of his or her own personal views, preferences,

and boundaries as a transgression liable to elicit anger from others. Alongside a tendency to feel unjustified guilt and shame, individuals with this history may also struggle with anger (as described earlier), either by being easily triggered to become angry or by not having access to their own anger.

2. **Emotional neglect or conditional love and approval**. If a child grows up receiving primarily conditional attention and praise for excelling (academically, athletically) or for being a "good" (helpful, compliant, etc.) boy or girl, this can lead to valuing oneself through achievements (doing) rather than who one is (being). Such a child can grow into an overly compliant, conflict-averse individual who continues to rely on the praise and validation of others, with a very limited sense of their own identity, needs, and boundaries. This often leads to over-functioning in adulthood, both at work and in relationships, a lack of self-care, and may put individuals at risk of burnout and illness.
3. **Parentification or being expected to take on caregiving or other duties.** When children are expected to act in more adult ways than they are developmentally ready for, such as caring often for younger siblings or for ill caregivers, or being expected to take on financial responsibilities at a very young age, this can be harmful to healthy development in a number of ways. First, the child who is required to abandon their own needs in order to take on responsibilities for others often internalizes the idea that the needs of others matter more than their own. They may carry this belief into adulthood, and experience guilt any time they attend to or prioritize their own needs, leading to avoidance of doing so. Additionally, if the child is expected to act more maturely than they are ready for, it will be difficult for them to sustain this successfully. For a child, falling short of these unrealistic expectations can lead to a belief of inadequacy and incapability, as they do not yet understand the complexity and unattainability of what is being asked of them.
4. **Emotional, physical, or sexual abuse, or neglect.** Growing up with a parent or caregiver who, due to mental health issues, addictions, or a maladaptive parenting style, belittles, manipulates, frequently criticizes or insults the child, instrumentalizes the child to meet their own needs, withholds love, attention and/or affection from the child, or is verbally, physically, or sexually abusive, can create deep

feelings of shame, as children often blame themselves when they are mistreated or ignored. This can create a lifelong sense of unworthiness and inadequacy, leading to a proneness to inappropriate self-criticism, self-blame, and shame. Sexual abuse, in particular, has a tendency to generate enormous guilt and shame in survivors for a variety of reasons (e.g., the cultural taboo on sex making it difficult to discuss the abuse, feeling blamed or unsupported when the abuse is disclosed, etc).

CASE EXAMPLE | "It was all my fault"

Jeanette was a 911 dispatcher in her second year in this role. She reached out for support after a particularly challenging work experience. A call came in relating to a child who had been seriously injured in an accident, and the caller was both emotionally upset and also did not speak English fluently and clearly. As a result, Jeanette struggled to input the information into the system as quickly as she would have wished. She obtained just enough information and prioritized the call correctly as the top-tier emergency response, and many first responder crews arrived on scene, but unfortunately, the child died en route to the hospital.

Following the call, Jeanette felt pressure in her chest, feelings of overwhelm, and above all, a profound sense of guilt and shame. She had to go home early following this call, as she could not concentrate. "I messed up and a kid died because of me," she kept telling herself, despite the reassurance of her co-workers and supervisor that she did everything she could. Jeanette reached out for therapy a few days after this incident, at the urging of her supervisor.

In therapy, she gradually acknowledged that she is prone to excessively taking responsibility for negative events that occur, both professionally and personally. She began to become more aware of the stress and pain that this generated in her life. Over the subsequent weeks, Jeanette worked hard in therapy to learn to differentiate between justified and unjustified guilt, developing the skill of self-compassion. Gradually, her guilt gave way to adaptive grief and finally to acceptance of the tragic outcome of the call.

Recommendations for Overcoming Maladaptive Guilt and Shame

1. **Create a responsibility pie.** A responsibility pie is a simple yet effective tool in CBT designed to address excessive self-blame regarding a specific situation. To use this tool, think of a situation for which you struggle with feelings of guilt. As a percentage, rate your initial feeling of responsibility for the event in question. Next, create a list of all the individuals and entities that also had some role in the outcome in question. Draw a circle (the "pie") and carve out sections for each of the entities responsible, including yourself. What do you notice? Oftentimes, when we reflect on all the individuals and collectives holding some responsibility for a specific outcome, our sense of our own responsibility for the situation (and associated guilt and shame) significantly diminish. The case example "Who Is to Blame?" (Chapter 27) illustrates this point.
2. **Imagine that the situation involved a friend or colleague and not yourself.** Imagine someone you are close to, and not you, experienced an identical situation. What would you say to help them see the situation in a way that does not generate guilt or shame? Try to offer yourself the same reassurance or gentle challenge. You might wish to use the ABCD framework (Chapter 15) to guide your reflection.
3. **Remember the common humanity of error and imperfection.** All human beings make mistakes, and it is only a matter of time before each of us makes an error or omission of some sort. Rather than generalizing from an event to a global judgment of your abilities or personality traits, make amends when possible and focus on what you can learn from and do differently in the future. This orientation fosters an ongoing commitment to growth through experiences, as opposed to contributing to feelings of shame, avoidance, and negative core beliefs about oneself.
4. **Consider the role of your early history (or other painful life experiences) in shaping your guilt and shame proneness.** If you struggle with frequently feeling guilt and shame, even when your behavior or conduct did not violate your own values and ethics, and despite being reassured by others that you are not responsible, consider whether this may be a protective tendency you picked up

earlier in your life in response to painful interpersonal circumstances. Consider seeking the support of a mental health professional to explore the origins of your feelings of guilt and shame if these pose challenges for you and you find this difficult to change.

Key Points

What is one thing you are taking away from reading this chapter?

____

Action Plan

What is one action you can take to improve your coping with guilt and shame?

____

CHAPTER 21

Understanding Sadness and Grief

Sadness and closely related emotions, including grief, helplessness, hurt, and disappointment, are the emotions that arise when we experience a loss of an important person or situation, or the loss of some other valued aspect of our lives, such as our physical health and vitality. These emotions can also arise in the context of very difficult circumstances and when we wish for reality to be different from the way it is. Sadness helps signal to us and others the need for care and support, prompting us to slow down, conserve energy, and process the situation and associated emotions. Feelings of sadness can be difficult to process and even to access for many people. The phrase "inhibited grief" has been used to describe the difficulty that some people develop in accessing and processing experiences of sadness, helplessness, and grief (Gantz, Gallagher-Thompson, & Rodman, 1992).

It is worth highlighting the "slow down" function inherent to sadness. For those of us in healthcare and first responder roles, occupations that rarely allow us to slow down and take care of our sadness, it is no wonder that many of us struggle with avoiding rather than processing our sadness. Frequent exposure to sad situations coupled with a heavy workload often means there is little time to slow down and process all the grief and loss inside of us. And many of us were neither taught nor modeled how to process sadness and loss in a healthy way. As a result, many individuals develop a variety of mechanisms to subdue the sadness, including developing secondary emotions (e.g., guilt, anger) that hide the more vulnerable primary emotions, overworking or being perpetually busy, detaching from their bodies, and using self-soothing strategies such as food, alcohol, or behavioral addictions.

We have already encountered some examples of first responders and healthcare professionals for whom grief became hidden and unprocessed following painful events. In Chapter 15, we met Ali, a paramedic who struggled with unjustified guilt for not being able to save the young victim of a car accident. By focusing on what he could or should have done differently in the motor vehicle collision call, Ali was, at least in part, avoiding his emotions of sadness and helplessness in response to having to watch a young woman die. While it caused Ali considerable distress to blame himself, the guilt also protected him from feeling completely helpless about what had taken place.

Patients often come into therapy with deep shame for crying. They try to contain their tears and maintain composure, and apologize profusely to me when tears come, even in the private therapy setting. It may surprise you, and it certainly surprises my patients, when I congratulate those who can feel their sadness and cry with ease when crying and grief are completely appropriate. It tells me that they are attuned to their own sadness and have managed to maintain access to crying— an incredibly healthy, helpful, natural release valve for our emotions, which helps our nervous system regulate. It is actually the people who struggle to access sadness and to cry that tend to have a longer and more challenging road to healing and recovery, at least in my experience.

To make matters more challenging, sadness and grief tend to be more subtle than anger, fear, or shame in the ways they manifest in the body. Sadness often shows up as heaviness or a mild ache in the chest, a feeling of weight on one's shoulders, or moisture in the eyes. Patients, including busy first responders and healthcare professionals, often have to really slow down and deliberately tune into their bodies to learn to notice and identify their sadness. If, like in the example of Mila, a female police officer later in this chapter, you have been disconnected from recognizing sadness for some time, this puts you at risk of long-term psychological distress. I will provide a list of concrete recommendations for addressing sadness and grief later in this chapter. In fact, many of the tools and strategies throughout this book— mindfulness of thoughts and feelings, reframing unhelpful thinking patterns, self-compassion practices, and radical acceptance, all directly or indirectly foster the processing of natural emotions, including grief and sadness. I encourage each of you to try to become more interested in and tolerant of your own sadness.

While sadness and grief are adaptive emotions, it is worth taking a moment to differentiate healthy expressions of sadness and grief from states of depression. The line between a natural, healthy state of sadness and a pathological one is not always clear in practice, but there are a couple of distinguishing features, in my view. To put it simply, sadness and grief are transient emotional states. The person who is grieving or experiencing sadness typically continues to function – at work, in caregiving duties such as parenting or eldercare, continues some self-care behaviors, and maintains some ability (even if temporarily blunted) to experience positive emotions – love for children, and pleasure from a subset of enjoyable activities. The depressed person, on the other hand, feels negative emotions, such as sadness, irritability, hopelessness, or numbness, most of the time, and this state lasts for a prolonged period of time without relief. It is often also hard for the depressed person to function and to do the everyday tasks of life, both at work and at home. The depressed person often experiences hopelessness about the future, self-criticism and feelings of worthlessness, and there is often a lack of self-care behaviors. The line between these two states becomes quite blurry in reality, as it is very possible and even common, after a major stressor or loss, to begin with adaptive grief and then have this gradually transform into a prolonged depressive illness.

You may be wondering what one needs to do following an upsetting event to process the grief without either suppressing it or allowing it to take over and turn into a depressive state. In my clinical experience, I have noticed one consistent difference between the folks for whom sadness or grief will be a transient state and those for whom it will become long-lasting. Those who continue to engage in healthy coping mechanisms, including physical exercise, mindfulness practices, hobbies, time spent with supportive others, and other meaningful and enjoyable activities, tend to recover more easily from states of grief and sadness.

On the other hand, those whose lives (and minds) become focused on the loss or stressor and who do not engage in self-care, connection with supportive others, and other healthy pursuits, are more at risk for the sadness to become persistent and impairing. The ability to step into and be with one's sadness on the one hand, while also being able to step out of it and still experience enjoyment, meaning, and connection, in my eyes depends on the trait of psychological flexibility, which can be understood as being open to feelings of grief without being stuck in and consumed by them (Kashdan & Rottenberg, 2010). Of note, many of the strategies described in this book are intentional practices that enhance psychological flexibility, and in doing so, support the development of greater psychological resilience and well-being.

As I write this chapter on the importance of accessing, expressing, and processing grief, I recall the many first responders and healthcare professionals who have, over the years, shared with me just how socially costly it is for them to express sadness at work. For many, there is fear of judgment and ridicule by peers should they lose emotional composure, even briefly. If this is true for you, then your workplace may not be the place where you can fully access and express your emotions. I still encourage you to acknowledge and name the emotions silently as they arise in you, including sadness and grief. You can make an internal commitment to make space and time for processing this emotion at a later point in time, when it is safer to do so. You can also, just for a moment, use self-compassion (Chapter 22) to validate and support the part of you that is hurting at this moment.

Then, at a later point when it feels safer to do this, whether in a therapy session, with a peer support staff member, in a candid conversation with a trusted colleague, friend, or spouse, you can more fully acknowledge, feel, and express your grief and sadness. Vulnerable sharing also tends to elicit validation from supportive others, which can provide a great deal of relief. Here are some additional recommendations for accessing and processing grief:

- **Reflect on past experiences of adversity.** Many of us carry unprocessed grief due to adversity and unmet needs from our childhoods. A wide range of events including feeling misunderstood by caregivers, not having our needs for nurturance met, being scolded by a harsh teacher, experiences of poverty or war, and experiences of teasing or rejection by peers can create deep grief for a child. These are experiences that, as children, we typically lack the skills to acknowledge and fully process when we are young. Additionally, many of us have faced painful experiences resulting in sadness, loss, and helplessness, either through our work or in our personal lives as adults. If a past event is very difficult to talk or think about, it is a sign that there may be unprocessed emotion needing to be addressed, which often includes grief. If you suspect that you have painful past events and emotions that need to be processed, I encourage you to prioritize this. If these events are difficult to talk and think about on your own, I encourage you to consider obtaining support and guidance from a mental health professional in accessing and processing these fully.
- **Reflect on whether there is a reality that you are struggling to accept.** In situations where you feel emotionally stuck, you may wish to ask yourself with curiosity, “Is there a reality here that I am avoiding

or refusing to accept?" The shift from rejecting to accepting a less-than-ideal reality, and the letting go of hope where there is little likelihood of change, is often accompanied by increased grief. For example, I have had many patients over the years describe feeling stuck in an unhappy job or romantic relationship, and cling to the hope that one day things will change dramatically, even when there is no evidence that change is forthcoming. When they shift into acceptance that the situation is unlikely to change, grief arises. Processing this grief helps deepen awareness of the reality of the given situation, and this often opens the door to new options and avenues for coping.

- **Be mindful not to rush through grief.** If the situation involves a significant loss of a person, a desired situation, or hope for another outcome, take time to reflect on the impact of the loss on you. We often try to move on from loss too quickly, without adequately making space to grieve what is no longer present in our lives. This does not mean stopping other aspects of your life, but it does mean slowing down and tuning in to support the parts of you that are still grieving.
- **Consider whether your anger (or guilt) may be masking sadness.** When we find ourselves angry with the actions or inactions of others or feeling unjustified guilt over what we did or did not do, feelings of disappointment, hurt, or grief may linger unprocessed underneath the surface. In such situations, take time to reflect on whether sadness may also be present. Learn to recognize where and how sadness tends to show up in your body. If sadness is present, offering yourself self-compassion and eliciting support and comfort from others may be helpful in fully honoring this emotion and the associated needs.
- **Lean on self-care, enjoyable activities, and social supports for coping.** As discussed earlier, it is crucial to continue to engage in activities that bring meaning, joy, and pleasure, and with people that foster a sense of being supported, understood and cared for, especially during times when we feel sad or are grieving. Often, the desire to be comforted and validated is a key need we have when we are sad. Connection with supportive others, including in therapy, also reminds us to tap into our self-compassion. These three elements—self-compassion, connection with supportive others, and making time for healthy, pleasant, meaningful, and enjoyable pursuits —are key to recovery from periods of sadness and grief.

- **Remember that grief is not linear.** One of the challenging things about grief and sadness is that the course of these emotions is not linear. Instead, many describe the process as "waves" that come and go in a fairly unpredictable manner, depending on life events as well as our own physical and emotional states. Be patient with yourself and try not to judge your own sadness and grief. If you find yourself crying over a loss from decades ago or a stressor that others around you seem far less affected by, it is still as important as ever to allow and acknowledge the emotion and to access self-compassion and external supports.
- **If you notice you are feeling sadness most of the time, even weeks after a stressor has subsided, consider talking to a professional.**. If it has been more than a couple of weeks since its onset, and sadness is taking up most of your waking hours, if you are struggling to function in your various roles and obligations, or if you are struggling to feel connected with your loved ones or to enjoy activities you previously liked, you may be beginning to enter into depression territory. There is no need to panic; this is a very common experience, especially when significant stressors or losses are present. However, it is best to err on the side of caution and speak openly with a healthcare provider or a mental health clinician. They will support you as you continue to process your emotions and ensure that you are headed for recovery rather than into a longer period of distress and impairment.
  Similarly, the emergence of any thoughts of harming or killing yourself that linger are indicators that this is not healthy, transient sadness and grief, but a potentially more problematic state that necessitates professional attention. If you experience these thoughts for any length of time, a prompt visit to a primary healthcare or mental health provider is warranted.

CASE EXAMPLE | Putting on a Brave Face

Mila was a police officer in her 40s working on patrol duties in a busy urban police service. She presented for therapy primarily for help with chronic irritability, at home and at work. She shared that she recently attended an emergency call wherein a 6-year-old child was seriously injured. Mila reported that, to her surprise and horror, while providing life-saving care to this child, she felt completely emotionally numb. She also reported that, gradually over the past fifteen years of policing, she has started to feel "either angry, or no emotions at all".

As therapy unfolded, Mila recalled the pressure she felt as one of the few young, female police officers working in her service at the time to prove herself to her predominantly male peers. She wanted very much for the male cops to see that she is "just as tough and capable" as any of them. She recalled feeling fear, horror, and fighting to hold back tears during particularly intense calls in her first few years of policing. She knew that if her peers saw her becoming emotional, they'd make fun of her and see her as too sensitive and emotionally fragile for police work. So gradually, Mila learned to "steel" herself and "stuff" her emotions. "The problem is," Mila said with a half-smile, "I've gotten so good at that, now even I myself can't seem to access my feelings."

We explored Mila's early life and its influences on her emotional processing style. Mila recalled that, as a sensitive child and only daughter in the family, her two older brothers played pranks on her to provoke an emotional reaction. There, too, she learned to appear "tough" and unaffected when she was upset. At other times, she used her explosive anger to put her brothers in their places when she had finally had enough. Mila decided that at this point in her life, she no longer wanted to be "tough"— she wanted to be able to feel things the way she did when she was a young woman.

Part of Mila's treatment involved emotionally processing painful emergency calls from early in her career. One particularly painful call she remembered involved trying to resuscitate an infant, and having paramedics rush him off still without a stable pulse. She recalled the cries of his distraught mother. Seeing this made Mila herself become tearful, but she fought to maintain composure so as not to lose face among the other officers on scene. In session, she was gently and slowly guided to notice the emotions arising in her body, such as the pressure of tears welling in her eyes. She reminded herself that right then, there was no need to push the sadness away and it is safe to make space for it to arise. Very gradually, over many sessions, she shifted from having no access to her emotions to recognizing and allowing them to arise and be expressed.

Despite this newfound attunement to her feelings, Mila found to her surprise that she continued to have the option to remain emotionally composed when she needed to, especially during emergency calls at work. In those situations, she named the emotions, acknowledged that the situation was painful, and made a silent commitment to herself to revisit it in therapy and on her own. She understood the importance of attending to her emotions and body, especially after stressful experiences. Not only was she better able to access her sadness and fear, but also re-gained access to feelings of excitement, love, ease and joy, as these began to show up more regularly and intensely in her life. She shared that after many years of feeling zombie-like and emotionally numb, she now felt like she was fully human and alive.

Key Points

What is one thing you are taking away from reading this chapter?

____

Action Plan

What is one way you can improve your coping with sadness and grief?

____

CHAPTER 22

Self-Compassion: Caring for Yourself While Caring for Others

One of the most essential skills to add to your toolkit for dealing with stressful situations is self-compassion. For those of us whose goal is to thrive in professions where we frequently confront the suffering, illness, and death of others, the skill of self-compassion is a non-negotiable.

Self-compassion has been defined as the willingness to be with one's own suffering without judgment, coupled with the motivation to support and help oneself. In my experience, many first responders and healthcare professionals respond to the suffering of others with compassion and a desire to help, yet respond to their own suffering with avoidance, minimization ("it's not that bad"), dark humor, or criticism ("what's wrong with me for feeling this way?"). The good news here is that first responders and healthcare professionals are often loving, deeply compassionate people. They know well how to be compassionate— they are just not used to seeing themselves, too, as both in need of and worthy of it.

It often comes as a surprise to my patients when I suggest that there is a gentler, healthier way to respond to themselves when they face difficulties. Many patients first react to the notion of self-compassion with skepticism and fear that it will diminish their motivation to grow and better themselves. If they've used self-criticism to push and motivate themselves, they fear that self-compassion will lead to laziness, complacency, or self-indulgent behavior. The concern is reasonable, but luckily unfounded. Treating oneself with compassion, recognizing the common humanity of both suffering and of making mistakes, and cultivating a focus on learning and growth, increases our psychological resilience, improves our emotional well-being, and allows us to recover from setbacks more quickly (Neff & Germer, 2017).

I introduce the skill of self-compassion to each and every one of my first responder and healthcare professional patients. I believe that careers involving complexity, heavy emotional and mental demands, and frequent stress require practitioners to find ways to nourish and sustain themselves in the face of these challenges. Self-compassion takes time and practice to develop, especially if it has not been a prominent way you have related to yourself until now. The good news is that if you commit to developing a more self-compassionate, supportive attitude internally, your relationship with yourself will likely improve, and this may lead to trickle-down effects on other aspects of your well-being, such as self-care and style of relating to others.

I have found that patients who work as first responders and healthcare professionals are also often very desensitized to the difficult and stressful nature of their work. From working long shifts, often with mandatory overtime, witnessing acute human pain (physical, emotional, and often both), constantly being reminded of mortality and the fragility of human life, carrying the weight of responsibility for the life and death of others, and having to make decisions with enormous consequences in moments, these roles involve significant stressors. When I suggest to my patients that their occupations are among the most emotionally taxing ones out there, it often takes them time to consider and accept this feedback. They are simply not used to thinking of their professions this way.

As you will see in the self-compassion break exercise below, the first step of self-compassion is once again mindfulness – mindfully tuning into the pain and suffering we are experiencing in the present moment. This step is already tough for many first responders and healthcare professionals because they have adapted to the chronic stress and demands of their lives by tuning out from their emotions and bodies on an ongoing basis (a mechanism described back in Chapter 4). We also covered in Chapter 18 the mechanism of experiential avoidance, the habitual turning away from distressing feelings, which is a common, understandable, but ultimately harmful response to one's own emotional distress. The alternative, tuning in, can be practiced using the more general mindfulness practices offered earlier in this book (Chapter 6), and then applied to tuning in specifically during experiences of struggle and suffering, which is the first step in the practice of self-compassion.

Once somatic and emotional awareness begins to strengthen in us, we become more acutely aware of moments when painful emotions, memories, and physical discomfort and pain are present. This is one of the costs of mindfulness— emotional and physical pain become more difficult to ignore and override. However, these moments provide an opportunity to nourish ourselves through validation, encouragement, and kindness. Two commonly used self-compassion exercises, the Self-Compassion Break and compassionate letter writing (Neff, n.d.) are completed as follows.

Practice Exercise: The Self-Compassion Break

Think of a situation in your life that is difficult, that is causing you stress. Call the situation to mind, and see if you can actually feel the stress and emotional discomfort in your body. Now, say to yourself:

1. This is a moment of suffering. That's mindfulness.
   Other options include: This hurts. Ouch. This is stress.
2. Suffering is a part of life. That's common humanity. Other options include: Other people feel this way. I am not alone. We all struggle in our lives. Now, place your hands over your heart and feel the warmth of your hands as they gently touch your chest. Or adopt the soothing touch you discovered felt right for you.
3. May I be kind to myself. You can also ask yourself, "What do I need to hear right now to express kindness to myself?" Is there a phrase that speaks to you in your particular situation, such as:
   - *May I give myself the compassion that I need*
   - *May I learn to accept myself as I am*
   - *May I forgive myself*
   - *May I be strong*
   - *May I be patient*

This practice can be used any time of day or night and will help you remember to evoke the three aspects of self-compassion when you need it most.

Practice Exercise: Compassionate Letter Writing

The second self-compassion practice to consider involves writing a self-compassionate letter to yourself. The self-compassionate letter could be to your current self, or to a past version of yourself during a particularly painful experience or period of time.

Here are some prompts to guide you in writing a self-compassionate letter.

Begin with kindness. Imagine you are writing to a dear friend who is struggling in the same way you are. Start by offering yourself gentle, kind words rather than criticism.

Example: "I know this is such a painful experience for you. I want you to know that you are not alone and that I care about your suffering."

Mindfully acknowledge the pain. Describe what you're feeling and going through right now (or what you went through at the time). Be honest, but non-judgmental.

Example: "I notice how hard you've been on yourself lately about [situation]. It makes sense that you feel this way, given how important this is to you."

Recognize common humanity. Remind yourself that suffering, mistakes, and imperfections are part of being human.

Example: "Everyone struggles at times and feels this kind of pain. You are not broken or different for feeling this way."

Offer support and encouragement. Write what you need to hear in this moment—words of reassurance, hope, or guidance.

Example: "I want you to remember that you are worthy of love and respect exactly as you are. I believe you can get through this. I am here for you."

Close with compassion. End the letter by expressing ongoing care and commitment to yourself.

Example: "I will keep showing up for you, even when things feel difficult. You deserve patience, kindness, and rest."

CASE EXAMPLE | Putting on a Brave Face (Continued)

In the previous section, we met Mila, the police officer who learned to suppress her emotions to appear tough and capable as a female in law enforcement. Later in therapy, Mila was asked to write a compassionate letter to her younger self, the version of herself that attended the pediatric call involving resuscitation of an infant. Here is what Mila's self-compassionate letter might sound like:

Dear Mila,

I know that you tried so hard to save that little baby, and that this was the first time you saw a baby on the verge of death. Your heart broke for him and for his mother, who was weeping uncontrollably. Yet, seeing your colleagues and supervisors on the scene, you knew you had to be tough. I know that was so hard and painful for you to put on a brave face and hold back your own tears. I'm sorry that you had to do that that day, and so many days since. I realize how hard it has been for you to be a woman in the police service, surrounded by men every day and having to prove yourself on each and every call. You are not alone in this struggle. The pressure to be tough is there for every cop, but it is so, so high for women. You have proven yourself as a tough, capable cop for the past 15 years. I am here to support you in reconnecting with your heart and emotions. You have nothing to prove to anyone anymore. Be kind to yourself and take care of yourself. Love, Mila.

Key Points

What is one thing you are taking away from reading this chapter?

____

Action Plan

What is one way you can increase your access to self-compassion?

____

CHAPTER 23

Radical Acceptance: Letting Things Be As They Are

Radical acceptance is the practice of acknowledging and accepting reality as it is. The practice is to let go of struggling or resisting against circumstances (Linehan, 2015). It is not an easy skill to learn. I consider it one of the most challenging ones to practice. With practice, however, radical acceptance can lead to a sense of increased peace and decreased suffering when faced with adversity. Radical acceptance has its philosophical roots in Buddhism. In Buddhism, accepting life as it is, even if it is not the way we wish it were, is one of the most central teachings. Radical acceptance serves as a bridge between psychological practices and ancient wisdom, offering a pathway to greater emotional resilience and psychological health even in the midst of significant challenges. Dr. Marsha Linehan, who became a Zen teacher before developing her renowned treatment, DBT, emphasized the power of radical acceptance throughout her treatment modality.

Radical acceptance is exquisitely challenging for most of us because when life throws a painful curveball our way in the form of an illness, a cheating spouse, being let go from our "dream job," or the loss of a child, every fiber of our being wants to control, deny, or blame someone. We may react to these stressors with anger, despair, and a profound sense of injustice, and in doing so, compound our suffering in response to the situation.

Radical acceptance is also a challenge because we often believe we can control our circumstances. I have found that first responders and healthcare professionals, individuals in quintessential helper and rescuer roles, struggle mightily with radical acceptance. In their work, first responders and healthcare professionals tend to lean into their sharp problem-solving abilities, take pride in their skills of helping, and excel at making situations turn for the better. The problem arises when all available problem-solving efforts have been exhausted, and the outcome remains suboptimal or even tragic. Sometimes, despite our best efforts, people will suffer, harm themselves, harm others, or die prematurely. In situations that defy resolution or where problem-solving is insufficient, a radically different approach is necessary to cope.

When we have done everything we can to help, ease suffering, or save a life, the healthiest thing to do, first, is to recognize that this is the case. This is more beneficial than persisting in a futile struggle or looking for some culprit to blame. Accepting the situation as both unchangeable and nobody's fault brings us into contact with the reality before us. This recognition frees up important emotional resources to support both ourselves and other people who are impacted by the situation.

To clarify, applying radical acceptance to a situation does not imply approval of the situation or behavior. It merely acknowledges that a situation is the way it is, that it is not in our control, and that despite this, we must find ways to cope with it. The example below involving a paramedic, Chris, and a challenging patient, Paul, illustrates how radical acceptance can be used by first responders and healthcare professionals when faced with challenging situations. Notice how, when Chris adopts a stance of radical acceptance toward the fact that he could not help Paul in the way he might like to given Paul's lifestyle and current choices, Chris becomes able to consider other ways to make a positive difference for Paul.

CASE EXAMPLE | Meeting Patients Where They Are

Chris, a mid-career paramedic, opened a therapy session by sharing a frustrating experience that had been troubling him. "We keep getting dispatched to the same guy, Paul," he told me. "He is in his late 60s, has a million chronic health issues, smokes like a chimney, and drinks a ton of alcohol. Anytime we suggest a trip to the hospital, he just refuses. He says he doesn't feel well, gets checked out, and then goes back to destroying himself. What a waste of time! He is just doing this because he is bored and lonely."

I've heard some version of this story many times in my office, from patients who are frustrated by the dire circumstances of their own patients and by the repeat users of emergency services. These are people who appear to choose unhealthy behaviors (poor diet, neglect of health conditions, substance abuse, etc) on the one hand, and frequently consume emergency and healthcare resources on the other. First responders and healthcare providers, like Chris, understandably feel powerless to really help in a meaningful way when faced with patients and situations that seem "beyond repair."

While exploring Chris's frustration with Paul, the underlying emotions of powerlessness, profound sadness, and hopelessness surfaced. As the concept of radical acceptance was introduced, Chris was curious and eager to feel less frustrated and angry the next time he was dispatched to Paul's home. He was particularly intrigued by the notion that he should shift some of his attention from Paul's needs to being compassionate toward himself in light of this sad, hopeless situation he was repeatedly exposed to. He was not used to turning toward his own emotions and suffering. As he became able to access self-compassion, he noticed himself become nourished and resourced by his own compassionate energy, and able to deal with Paul with more kindness and grace. He was gradually able to shift from wanting to drastically fix Paul's life situation to simply viewing Paul as a fellow human who was suffering, and doing the best he could given his circumstances.

Chris noticed with surprise that the frustration, judgment, and pressure to "rescue" or drastically force Paul to change began to diminish. As a result of the shift, Chris was able to show up in a more compassionate way when interacting with Paul; they even began to share some jokes. Seeing that Chris had a genuine interest in getting to know him, Paul began sharing a little more about his life and what he had gone through while growing up. Hearing of Paul's history of poverty and profound neglect, as his parents struggled with substance use challenges, Chris began to understand why Paul seemed to care so little about his own health and well-being. Chris was sad for Paul but recognized that, in his role as a paramedic, he could only do so much for the man, as their interactions were necessarily brief and focused on current health concerns. Nevertheless, Chris felt that by providing care with patience, grace, compassion, and even a bit of humor, he was making a difference for Paul. Gradually, Chris admitted timidly that he began to actually look forward to seeing Paul, for whom he had come to care deeply.

Here are a few recommendations to begin to bring more radical acceptance into your day-to-day life:

1. **Start small.** Try to practice radical acceptance in situations that create only modest amounts of distress for you, such as running a few minutes behind schedule, dropping and breaking a dish, or delays due to unexpected traffic.
2. **Cultivate radical acceptance in your self-talk.** Identify unhelpful thinking patterns that contribute to your distress, and practice responding with acceptance in your internal dialogue. This may include reassuring phrases such as, "This situation sucks, but it is not the end of the world," "Everybody runs late from time to time," "This too shall pass," and "This is not worth getting worked up about," or simply, "It's okay." Aside from helping to reduce emotional arousal, this type of self-talk reminds us of the common humanity of struggle—a key tenet of self-compassion.
3. **Focus on sensations and emotions in the body.** This is one of those times when being attuned to the body and ideally having an existing mindfulness practice are both very helpful. In addition to bringing acceptance into your thinking, as outlined above, when you notice frustration or resistance arising, you may also notice your body tensing up. This is the body's way of saying, "no!" to the present moment. As you notice this, try to take deep breaths and release some of the tension built up in your body. This is most effective when paired with the acceptance-oriented thoughts and affirmations suggested above.
4. **Reinforce your own radical acceptance practice positively**. Recognize places in your life wherein you find radical acceptance challenging, and honestly evaluate how your non-acceptance is negatively impacting your well-being in these situations. Set a personal growth goal to be more accepting of the challenging circumstances that inevitably arise. Acknowledge and praise yourself for practicing this skill when facing day-to-day challenges.
5. **Help yourself accept situations using self-compassion**. People often have the mistaken notion that radical acceptance means becoming robot-like and having no emotion in response to painful situations. This is not at all the case. In fact, radical acceptance is very often

associated with painful emotions that arise when we stop fighting to make situations or people change. In radical acceptance, we often have to come to terms with the loss of a person, situation, or the hope for changing a particular outcome. This is often accompanied by negative emotions, such as grief. In such situations, self-compassion and radical acceptance mutually reinforce one another – radical acceptance helps us see the reality that is, and self-compassion allows us to support ourselves through the painful emotions that arise in response to the the difficult reality we are facing.

Reflection

- Can you think of one or two day-to-day situations that cause you frustration or distress? Which of the strategies described can help you bring more radical acceptance to these situations?
- Next, identify a more significant situation, personal or professional, where you are finding it challenging to accept reality. Which of the strategies described can help you bring acceptance to this situation?
- How can increased radical acceptance benefit you in coping with difficulties that arise? Are there any costs to practicing radical acceptance when facing these challenges?

Key Points

What is one thing you are taking away from reading this chapter?

___

Action Plan

what is one way you can increase your capacity for radical acceptance when confronting difficulties in your life?

___

CHAPTER 24

Chronic Exposure to Suffering and Death

Suffering and death are inevitable aspects of human life. We will all face them in some way, in what can become some of the most difficult and painful experiences of our lives. First responders and healthcare professionals encounter suffering and death regularly, and these encounters carry some unique demands and challenges by virtue of our professional roles. Specifically, when we witness suffering or death as professionals, those around us may expect us to step in and help. The pressure on us to somehow save and rescue, physically or emotionally, can be truly enormous, and can come both from those around us and from ourselves.

The reality is that, in many situations, there is not very much we can do to help. When tragedies happen under our professional watch and we are powerless to change outcomes, the experience can leave us feeling helpless, bereft, and guilty. I have witnessed time and again the profound toll such situations can take. We may have to witness the patients and people we serve, for whom we care deeply, suffer and die, suddenly during surgery, gradually from cancer, or by their own hand through suicide. We witness their distraught loved ones in acute grief and pain. These experiences trigger our sadness and compassion, and serve as reminders of the fragility and impermanence of each of our lives, and the lives of our loved ones. I believe these are some of the riskiest experiences for first responders and healthcare professionals, perhaps not physically, but certainly psychologically. This is because, if not processed effectively, being so close to this type of suffering and pain has great potential to create long-term psychological distress.

Now, it is true that many of us would rather think of more upbeat topics in our day-to-day lives than death and suffering. You may even notice some inner resistance to continuing to read this section. This is understandable. These topics can be scary, heavy, and painful, and we may try to avoid them whenever possible. Yet, the strategy of avoiding thinking, feeling, and talking about death, grief, and suffering can only take each of us so far. Life events can, without warning, thrust the realities of suffering and death into sharp focus.

As professionals, the avoidance of thinking and talking about death can negatively impact our ability to be fully present with those dying. It can also reduce opportunities to have healthy discussions and share about coping and grief. For those of us in healthcare and first responder roles, who cannot avoid and must confront death frequently in our work, avoidance leaves us more isolated in navigating the emotional intensity and the efforts to make sense of the experiences involving suffering or death that we witness through our work. It is thus important for everyone, but especially for those of us who encounter suffering and death routinely in our work, that we find ways to face these topics individually and in our professional communities.

Much has been written about death in philosophy, medicine, and, of course, in the spiritual traditions. I recognize that some of you may already have a framework—religious, scientific, philosophical—for understanding suffering and death. Many of the patients I work with have not reflected on these existential themes and struggle to make sense of events that evoke them, as I have in the past. I was brought up learning the Judeo-Christian takes on death and the afterlife, like many of you. As a child, due to circumstances that thrust suffering and death into my awareness at a young age, I grappled with this reality and wished for but struggled to find any framework that really "fit" for me. The religious and the scientific viewpoints I was exposed to early in life did not provide me with a satisfactory framework for the suffering, injustice, and deaths that occurred around me.

As I matured and later became a clinical psychologist, the suffering and grief of my patients and my own forced me to confront these themes more deliberately and systematically. My own thinking about life, death, suffering, and impermanence has been greatly influenced by teachings from Eastern (mainly Buddhist) spirituality. Of course, I cannot tell you exactly how to make sense of suffering and death, since what fits for me may not fit for you. I simply invite you to reflect, read, and discuss these topics whenever possible. Do not wait for a crisis to face these realities. I am hopeful that while this section may be a difficult read, you will find some ideas and suggestions worth holding onto and exploring further as you confront suffering and death in your line of work.

This section broadly introduces reflections on coping with suffering and death from various angles, including biographical, philosophical, and spiritual perspectives. The focus will then shift to the kinds of experiences that cause a great deal of suffering for first responders and healthcare professionals. Some of the most common themes that I have seen in my work include challenges tolerating the intense pain we witness in others, the self-blame and guilt that can arise when our efforts to help do not "work," and the unique set of challenges, pain, and guilt that are often triggered when a death of someone we love or care for occurs by suicide.

Reflection

- How do you currently make sense of situations involving prolonged suffering, especially when there is no prospect of recovery?
- How do you make sense of the suffering and death of children?
- What are the situations relating to suffering and death in your professional role that have challenged you the most? What about in your personal life? How do these impact you?
- What steps have you taken and what resources have you tried to aid your coping with these? What has been helpful and what has not?

Key Points

What is one thing you are taking away from reading this chapter?

___

Action Plan

What is one action you can take to foster reflection or helpful discussion about suffering and death?

___

Acceptance of Death: An Enormous Challenge

A prominent theme in the material I have read on death is an invitation to work to accept the reality of death as a natural, inevitable part of life. Marcus Aurelius, Roman Emperor and Stoic philosopher, once stated, "You could die at any moment. Don't waste your time" (Aurelius, ca. 180 CE/2002). A famous Buddhist teacher, Ajahn Chah, is similarly quoted as saying, "If you do recollect death regularly, you will cease to harm others" (Chah, 2018).

Working to accept death as a natural, inevitable part of life for all of us is not easy, but it does have a number of psychological benefits. First, when a death occurs, even if it seems premature, we may be less likely to respond with horror and a belief that some cosmic error has occurred, or that it is an unjust tragedy. Such thought processes are not effective in the sense that they amplify, rather than diminish, our emotional pain and suffering. And, when we do not take for granted that we or our loved ones have many more years or decades of life remaining, we may find it easier to appreciate, value, and be more discerning in how we spend this precious, finite resource called time.

As you reflect on these ideas, you might be thinking, "Isn't it antithetical to the helping professions to simply accept death, rather than to treat illness, minimize suffering, and keep people alive? Isn't preventing suffering and preserving life the very essence of our professions?" While it may seem counterintuitive to develop an acceptance of death, we find a dialectic here, the juxtaposition of opposites. Each time we encounter suffering or the prospect of death we can and should use our professional skills to help, serve, and support in any way we can. At the same time, we must work to accept that suffering and death will occur despite our best efforts. Rather than resisting this reality or looking for someone to blame, a stance of acceptance (Chapter 23) helps us see the situation most clearly. This clear vision facilitates our ability to find other ways of being of service, through acts that may include offering comfort to the dying or their loved ones, or simply bearing witness to the unfolding events with care and compassion. This may feel less heroic than what we wish to be able to do, but it has great potential to make a deep, lasting impact on those facing a painful, difficult time.

Having witnessed loved ones passing away after a lengthy period of suffering, and from speaking to many working in healthcare and first responder roles, it is also worth remembering that for many who are preparing to die, especially if they have suffered greatly due to old age, illness, or injury, the end of this life represents the welcome ending of a painful chapter. While we are generally conditioned to view death universally as a tragedy or failure of some sort, and while the loved ones of the deceased may not yet be ready to let go of their beloved, for many dying individuals, the body has truly become a burden and source of suffering. In these cases, death is not a tragedy, but a welcome reprieve from suffering. In our effort to be of service, we must be quite careful not to project our own ideas about suffering and death onto those we work with. Many may already have found their own effective way to coexist with these realities, even if their perspectives look quite different from our own.

And, even though confronting suffering and death may be "in our job descriptions," we must recognize how emotionally taxing and painful these situations are, especially when encountered frequently. Death is a reality to be accepted; that is true. But serving in professional roles where we witness death frequently, including the deaths of young people and in violent or tragic circumstances, exacts a heavy emotional toll. When we have done everything we can for a person suffering or facing death, it is an important practice to turn some of our resources inward in order to care for ourselves. Let us try to show up compassionately with a desire to support ourselves in the same way we bring these qualities to the service of others. Through recognizing suffering and supporting ourselves and our peers in the context of painful situations involving the suffering and death of others, we ensure that we can continue to bring our full selves to the challenging work we do.

CASE EXAMPLE | Caring for the Caregiver

Vivian was a late-career social worker who came to therapy for help with processing the death of her mother. As an only child, she looked after her mother for the past decade, as her mother, a woman well into her 90s, declined physically and cognitively following a stroke. A year had passed since her mother died, and Vivian was still very much struggling with low mood, frequent disturbing dreams involving her mother, and feelings of guilt and shame. As many mental health practitioners do when seeking therapy, Vivian also shared that she felt great shame for coming to therapy. As a mental health professional, she believed that she ought to know exactly how to go through this milestone in her life on her own, and yet she felt stuck.

As we unpacked the many thoughts and emotions evoked by her mother's passing, many different themes came up. Her mother's death put Vivian in direct touch with her own fears of aging, dependency, and eventual death. While she knew consciously that she had taken good care of her mother, she also at times felt that she had not done "enough" to ease her mother's suffering and loneliness, or to advocate for her within the medical system.

Finally, and most difficult for Vivian, was acknowledging how much of a burden it had been to care for her mother for an entire decade. She shared, tentatively at first, how depleting and sad it was to see her mother decline gradually into profound dementia, and the fact that when her mother passed, alongside the intense grief, she also felt equally intense relief.

In therapy, her experience of the dialectic of grief and relief was normalized. Vivian learned that it is an incredibly common experience, especially among caregivers of individuals with significant, progressive illnesses, such as her own mother's vascular dementia. She learned to gradually stop judging herself for what she had not done (and for her emotions) and instead validate and reinforce herself for all she had done for her mother during her mother's vulnerable final years. She was shocked to hear that many children, in her place, do much less for their ailing parent. She learned to hold both her grief and relief with self-compassion and see herself as having been a loving, albeit imperfect, daughter.

Finally, she was able to overcome her avoidance and began to acknowledge and work through her own fears of becoming completely dependent on others, and of becoming so cognitively impaired that she would not be able to recognize even her loved ones, like her mother had in her final years. She also began to verbalize and hold with compassion her grief for her own aging and fear of her own death, which, as she entered her mid-60s, felt not all that far away. This led to difficult but productive conversations with her husband and adult sons about her own end-of-life wishes. This also galvanized her intention to make the most of her remaining years by enjoying them and positively impacting the lives of those closest to her.

Key Points

What is one thing you are taking away from reading this chapter?

____

Action Plan

What is one way you can support yourself when you face situations involving suffering and death?

____

CHAPTER 25

How to Support Someone Who Is Suffering or Dying (and Support Yourself in the Process)

Many of us will be in a position to support a person facing death, either personally or professionally, at some point in our lives. In this section, I will share some thought-provoking ideas from prominent writers of various orientations, including philosophy, spirituality, and biographical accounts, on how to best support and be present with someone facing death. We will then examine what might hinder our ability to be fully present and supportive in this way and explore strategies to overcome these obstacles.

In his book, *Staring at the Sun: Being at peace with your own mortality*, Dr. Irvin Yalom, psychiatrist and author, shares the following advice as to how to be present with a person who is dying: "Empathy is the most powerful tool we have in our efforts to connect with other people; It is the glue of connection," and "connection is paramount. Whether you are a family member, a friend, or a therapist: Jump in. Get close in any way that feels appropriate. Speak from your heart. Reveal your own fears. Improvise. Hold the dying one in any way that offers comfort. Sheer presence is the greatest gift you can give someone facing death." (Yalom, 2008).

In his moving autobiography, Dr. Paul Kalanithi, a neurosurgeon who was diagnosed and later died from lung cancer while in his 30s, shared a very similar perspective: "The physician's duty is not to stave off death or return patients to their old lives, but to take into our arms a patient and family whose lives have disintegrated and work until they can stand back up and face, and make sense of, their own existence." (Kalanithi, 2016)

For those of us who work with individuals facing death, it is readily apparent that people face death very differently. Some may be at peace and ready for death, and we may struggle to comprehend their equanimity. Others may struggle immensely with issues such as unresolved hurts and traumatic experiences, regrets about what was said, done, or left unsaid, fear and concern for their loved ones, and fear of what's in store for them after they die. Similarly, loved ones may appear calm and accepting, shocked, relieved, or present with raw grief, sorrow, or anger. I have heard many times from my patients that the moment of providing a terminal diagnosis or a death notification to loved ones, and the floodgates of raw emotion that follow, are experiences that can cause immense emotional distress for healthcare professionals and first responders. I am afraid that there is nothing I can say to make these professional experiences pain-free; it is human to feel distress when we witness another in enormous pain. Even so, I offer you a few recommendations to consider if your work includes supporting someone who is dying, or someone whose loved one has died.

- **Remember that people may have vastly different reactions to death and dying.** Some remain eerily stoic, others appear shocked and dissociated, while others react in an effusively emotional way to situations involving death. Notice any judgments of the person or situation ("this shouldn't have happened") that arise within you and try to let these go in favor of radical acceptance. It is helpful to recall that most of us are with a person for a relatively brief snippet of time, and therefore are not privy to witnessing their grief unfold and resolve, something that can take considerable time.
- **Notice the thoughts and emotions that arise within you during the situation, acknowledge them and soothe yourself with self-compassion**. Employ kind and supportive self-talk, such as "Ouch, it is so painful to witness this mother's grief." Acknowledge and name your emotion. Commit to taking time to be with your own emotional reactions, either alone or with a supportive colleague, friend, or therapist. We are human and are inevitably affected by the unbridled pain we witness. If you are finding an event of this nature particularly painful, consider taking a little time away from work to allow yourself some time to process it fully.

- **Be mindful of the well-intentioned, but often ineffective, desire to rescue the person from their painful feelings or experiences.** As compassionate people, we are, of course, inclined to try to say something to fix a painful situation, offer hope or reassurance, or soothe the other person's distress. While well-intentioned, this tendency may prematurely direct and control the fear and grief of the other person. Paradoxically, holding space for and validating (i.e., reflecting that the emotion is valid) their current reaction is likely to be more helpful than any effort to guide or soothe. Statements such as, "I can appreciate how scary this must be for you," "I am so sorry you are facing this right now," and "It's okay to cry—I am here for you if you need me," can go an enormous way in helping the other person unburden themselves, offering significant relief and allowing healing to occur at its natural pace. It is best to pay attention to how the person themselves is speaking about the situation, the words they are using, and take cues from them on what to speak about (e.g., some may wish to discuss their feelings about dying, while others would rather talk about the football game). Taking cues from them and following, rather than leading, shows your respect and humility in the face of their unique processing of what is taking place and what is still to come.
- **Anticipate, acknowledge, and attend to your own grief, anger, horror, or other painful reactions to what you have witnessed.** Whether you are a physician facing the death of a patient, a paramedic or cop witnessing the death of a young person, or a firefighter having to deliver a death notification to loved ones, it is too easy to believe that, simply because the death is within a professional context, you would not have intense emotional reactions to it. We are, first and foremost, human. We form attachments to the people we work with over time, and often it is our care for others that inspires us to do this work. We often feel deeply for those we serve and we are moved by their grief and suffering. Following a painful event involving a death, take time to take stock of your reactions to the death, practice self-validation and self-compassion. If possible, acknowledge your emotions with compassion as the situation unfolds, or

soon thereafter if that is not possible. Try to give yourself extra opportunities to rest, connect with others, and experience positive emotions in the aftermath of an emotionally taxing event involving suffering or death.

- **Try to take some comfort in impermanence.** The person in front of you may be suffering acutely in this moment, and this may be very painful for you to witness. In such moments, it is helpful to remember that this suffering is impermanent. Hold onto hope that this person's situation will improve and that they will find comfort and healing from what is so painful for them right now. People can overcome and heal from immense adversity. Recalling this and staying hopeful may help the current situation feel more tolerable to witness.
- **If a situation lingers with you and you find yourself having a hard time recovering from it, seek support**. Talk to trusted peers, seek peer support at work, and consider speaking with a therapist if the event and emotions linger for you. Try not to judge yourself for feeling this way; it is simply a testament to the fact that you are a warm-hearted human and to how deeply you care. These intense situations can create lingering distress in the professionals who perform these difficult functions. A few sessions with a qualified clinician can often help fully process the experience and reduce its impact in the long term.

Facing Your Own Grief to Support Others Through Grief

I have noticed time and time again how much our own memories, beliefs, fears, and other unexamined emotional "stuff" related to suffering and death can get in the way of the open, calm, and compassionate stance that Drs. Yalom and Kalanithi described in their writings. Caring professionals often struggle to truly adopt this stance if they have not yet processed their own suffering and grief from past losses and adversity, as this can more easily be triggered by witnessing suffering and death professionally. This is one way avoidance of these topics impacts our ability to be fully present with others experiencing similar situations. This is why therapy, and the skill of self-compassion in particular, are of such central importance for first responders and healthcare providers, and why I return to these skills again and again throughout this book.

In my experience, once a first responder or healthcare professional has processed their own past suffering, overcomes the tendency to blame or criticize themselves, and incorporates the skill of self-compassion, it becomes much easier for them to hold space for the suffering of another in the same supportive, compassionate, non-judgmental manner. Yet, I see many first responders and healthcare professionals get stuck in a paradoxical place—they strive to live a life of service and find it easy to access a helping, compassionate stance toward others. At the same time, they profoundly neglect their own suffering, or worse, compound it with habitual self-criticism and self-neglect. The good news is that this book provides many strategies for attuning to our bodies, acknowledging the emotions we may have been avoiding, and offering ourselves nourishing mindfulness and self-compassion practices. The not-so-good news is that the shift to recognize and treat oneself as worthy of compassion is not easy, especially if this is very different from how you are used to relating to yourself. For many, this transition requires help from a therapist.

I encourage each of you to take time to process your own past and present suffering as mindfully and lovingly as possible, on your own, or with the help of a clinician. Unprocessed emotions related to losses, experiences with abandonment, and fears of suffering or death can be easily triggered by the suffering or death in the lives of those we serve. The more unprocessed emotion we carry within us, the more difficult it will be to provide a spacious, compassionate, calm presence to support those around us when they suffer, because when our own pain is triggered, we lose objectivity and equanimity. Our ability to see the present situation and the needs of those before us becomes obscured by our own pain.

Thich Nhat Hanh made this point eloquently in his writings, stating, "when you are compassionate with yourself, you are able to be compassionate with others. If you are not able to be compassionate with yourself, then how can you be compassionate with others?"

(Hanh, 1997). Dr. Jack Kornfield, psychologist and author, echoed this stance, stating, "If your compassion does not include yourself, it is incomplete." (Kornfield, 1993). As a psychologist, I agree with the emphasis on having "done our own work" in order to be able to effectively support others. So, if you are serving in a profession in which you will encounter suffering, pain, and death in others, take the time to process the pain, suffering, and grief in yourself, which may become an impediment to true presence and compassion with others.

CASE EXAMPLE | Tolerating the Pain of Another

Marko, a paramedic in his late 20s, came to therapy for support after a particularly difficult call. A woman had sustained severe burns and was writhing and yelling in agony throughout the time Marko was caring for her. He had, as per his training, attempted to provide various pain control interventions, but she did not respond to the pain medication and her suffering continued. Marko experienced enormous guilt and shame that she suffered this way and that he could not help her.

What would you say to Marko if he were sitting in your office?

During our sessions, Marko acknowledged that he was consciously aware that he had done everything possible and that his interventions could not work for every patient. At the same time, he could not shake the feeling that, as the medic in charge of this patient's care, he was responsible for the fact that she had to suffer this intensely. Marko felt stuck and deeply affected by this call, which led him to doubt whether he wanted to stay in this challenging profession.

Marko acknowledged that he was prone to taking excessive responsibility for the experiences of his patients, and we explored the roots of this tendency in his early life. He recognized that this tendency is unfair and causes him emotional distress to the point that continuing to work as a paramedic is very challenging. But he also endorsed believing that it made him a more thorough, responsible medic, and was unsure whether he would ever be able to change this about himself, and whether he even wanted to in the first place. Over time, this belief shifted as Marko realized that this belief was not an asset but a detriment to his well-being, hindering his ability to be an emotionally resilient, compassionate medic.

Through months of therapy, Marko gradually learned alternative ways of responding in such situations, including the important skills of radical acceptance and self-compassion. He was intrigued by self-compassion, realizing that this stance had never even occurred to him, and he had not seen self-compassion modeled by anyone in his life. He experienced profound relief as he began soothing and comforting himself when he was confronted with the suffering of his patients, or his own, in response to various stressors in his life.

Marko worked to develop trust in the resilience of the people he served to overcome the suffering of the present moment. In situations where he was helpless to ease the suffering of a patient, as in the case with the patient with severe burns, he practiced reminding himself that their intense pain and suffering would likely subside quite soon, when transferred to the hospital setting, where more options existed to help. This comforted Marko and helped him tolerate the moment with less distress. He also learned to take pride in the efforts he took to help the woman, including the quick and safe way he and his partner transported her to the hospital, and the gentle and reassuring way he treated her when she was in his care. He had often overlooked and taken for granted his gifts of sensitivity and skill in putting patients at ease. He was reminded to take pride in these time and time again, and eventually began to notice and take pride in both his technical skills as a paramedic and the interpersonal skills of staying calm and offering genuine compassion to those he served through his work.

In later therapy, Marko remarked that the skills of acceptance and self-compassion helped him become an even more patient, emotionally attuned and compassionate paramedic. When he began to use these new skills, his own emotional distress no longer got in the way of opening his heart to his patients and peers.

CASE EXAMPLE | Pediatric Death

Nadia and Ivana were two paramedics who were dispatched to an intense call involving a toddler who had drowned in the pool in the family's backyard. They, along with additional first responders from the local police and fire services arrived on scene, took many life-saving measures, but tragically, they were unable to resuscitate the child, who passed away on the scene. All of the first responders on scene were, in various ways and to differing degrees, deeply impacted by the event, though some of them were able to recover more quickly and completely than others. Let us now examine Ivana and Nadia's differing inner narratives about the event that transpired, and how each narrative is likely to impact their recovery from this call.

Nadia's self-talk: "How on earth did the kid get to the yard without the parents noticing? Man, he was so little and there was no adult in sight. They didn't even have a gate around the pool. How can people be so careless?"

"I wonder if we had gotten on scene a few minutes earlier, whether we could have saved him. Maybe, if we hadn't gotten stuck on the busy road on the way, we could have saved him. Damn, we should have gotten here faster. Maybe he could have had a chance then."

Ivana's self-talk: "That little boy was so tiny. His little body was so limp when the firefighters pulled him out that it was clear then that he probably wouldn't make it. He must have thought it would be fun to go in for a swim. Poor little guy. Couldn't get back out. I hope he didn't suffer."

"How awful for the parents too...the mom seemed inconsolable. Of course she was. How do you even recover from something like this? Man, I hope he didn't suffer for too long. What a tragedy."

Can you spot the subtle differences in the two ways of making sense of a tragic outcome? Which of the narratives do you think represents a healthier stance?

Nadia's reactions, filled with bewilderment and anger, are understandable. However, unfortunately, her way of making sense of this call demonstrates several common ways people can get stuck when making sense of difficult events. This includes preoccupation with open-ended questioning in ways that are difficult to resolve, anger toward others, and a feeling of personal responsibility and guilt for the outcome (Chapter 20). All of these ways of thinking can impede the natural recovery process, potentially leading to long-term psychological distress. Open-ended questions that are difficult, if not impossible, to answer, such as "how could this happen?" and "if only we had arrived sooner, could this have been prevented?" are a way many get stuck in cyclical, intrusive thought processes following a tragedy.

Because our brains do not like unanswered questions, the mind returns to the questions again and again, generating more and more possibilities, but can provide no real solutions or resolution. When working with patients who are stuck in such questioning, I find it helpful to support them in generating an answer to their question using the available information and then redirecting their attention to the present moment. For example, in response to Nadia's question, "how could this happen?" she might generate a response such as, "the tired mom made a tragic error, taking her eyes off her toddler for just a minute or two, and this decision will likely be one she regrets for the rest of her days."

Anger and guilt in relation to someone or some event can be kept alive indefinitely through beliefs, such as Nadia's judgment (and anger) toward the child's parents. If I were Nadia's psychologist, I would try to help her reframe the thoughts that produce anger (or guilt) using strategies such as the ABCD framework (Chapter 15). This, in my experiences, facilitates access to the primary emotion(s) beneath the anger. Often, in response to events like this, judging the self as having done something wrong or judging others as somehow to blame helps keep primary sadness and helplessness out of the person's awareness. Yet, these unprocessed primary emotions linger unprocessed and contribute to psychological distress. First responders and healthcare professionals who, like Nadia, have faced a tragedy, often find it helpful to access and acknowledge with compassion these more vulnerable emotions, including grief and helplessness to change the outcome. I imagine that this approach would bring Nadia relief, help her access support and validation by others, and ultimately would bring her closer to acceptance of this tragic call and its outcome.

Ivana's reaction, on the other hand, is more conducive to feeling the primary emotions related to the tragedy, in this case, sadness and helplessness for the tragic death of a child. Ivana's narrative, too, is suggestive of emotional pain, as would be the case for most who witness such an event. But Ivana's narrative is free of blame. She has started to process her sadness for the child's suffering and death, and for the heartbreak of his parents. It will likely take time, but her grief can proceed unimpeded by secondary processes like blame or questioning. By acknowledging her sadness and directing self-compassion toward her own feelings of grief, she will be supporting herself in the recovery process. In addition, her natural, primary emotions of sadness and grief are more likely to generate support and comfort from others (as compared to Nadia's anger), which may further expedite Ivana's healing and recovery.

Key Points

What is one thing you are taking away from reading this chapter?

____

Action Plan

What is one way you can support yourself when you encounter suffering and death in your work?

____

CHAPTER 26

Deaths by Suicide: An Emotional Minefield

Of all the different types of deaths we encounter, both professionally and personally, deaths by suicide represent one of the most difficult to cope with. In part, the profound psychological impact of a suicide of a colleague, patient, family member, or friend likely comes from the fact that suicide goes against the life-preserving drive within each living being. The act of suicide contradicts this, and those left behind often get stuck in asking "why?" or "how could they?" Many struggle to comprehend the decision to voluntarily end one's life, and in their desperation to make sense of the tragedy, many often also create narratives that blame themselves somehow for the tragic outcome. We have seen that self-blame is a common way of responding to the feelings of powerlessness that arise in tragic situations, and the suicides of those we are close to (or those we care for) are a prime trigger for self-blame and debilitating guilt.

Many patients over the years have spoken to me about their struggles following a suicide, whether it be of a relative, colleague, or patient. When a person completes suicide, family members, friends, and professionals who were involved in the person's care often experience intense guilt, shame, and self-doubt about whether they have done everything possible to support the person who has died. The sense of having failed can be intense and overwhelming. We may begin to believe that had we said or done something specific, we could have prevented the tragedy. It is natural to want to understand, or to mentally undo what has happened, but this is a way we can get stuck psychologically, leading to long-lasting distress.

The trouble is that in retrospect, we can easily convince ourselves that some sequence of steps of ours could have prevented a suicide. Yet, we have absolutely no way of knowing if events would have transpired the way we imagine. The more we become convinced that we had the power to intervene and save, and failed to do so, the more guilt sets in. In the most extreme cases, it can drive survivors to leave the caring professions, seeing themselves as unfit to continue, and some even begin to feel suicidal urges of their own, besieged by feelings of guilt and remorse.

Even we mental health professionals, who are trained in and engage in ongoing risk assessment, are not able to predict or prevent all suicides. With all of the societal and medical efforts to reduce suicide rates, we still tragically lose 4500 people annually in Canada to suicide (Government of Canada, 2024). A significant proportion of attempted or completed suicides do not involve lengthy planning by the person, with the suicide attempt arising in an impulsive, unplanned way (e.g., Simon et al., 2001). Let us take a moment to consider, if the deceased person themselves did not know their suicide attempt was going to take place, whether there is any fairness in family, friends, or healthcare professionals believing that they should have been able to foresee or prevent this from happening.

On the other hand, some people do plan in advance to end their lives. The causes for this tragic act are often very complex and multifaceted – traumas, life stressors, physical health difficulties, injuries and disabilities, addictions, social isolation, and mental health difficulties can all play a role. It is thus overly simplistic and likely not realistic to believe that "if only I had called him more," or "if only we had not had a fight earlier that week," the suicide would not have happened. And, not only are these beliefs often not grounded in fact, but holding onto them can create unimaginable, long-term psychological distress in those left behind. In reality, it can be almost impossible to truly know the exact reasons for the suicide. The person themselves may not even have known exactly why they wanted to die or what it would have taken for them to have chosen a different course of action.

Additionally, if a person is truly determined to end their life via suicide, they do not typically make their suicidal thoughts and plans known to those around them. This tragically takes away the ability of those around the individual to help find relief or appropriate supports before it is too late. The takeaway here is that in both impulsive and planned suicides, there are often a multitude of factors that make it nearly impossible for anyone to successfully prevent the event from happening.

A principal goal I keep in mind when working with individuals struggling with a completed suicide is the goal of promoting grieving. How this is done depends on what exactly is getting in the way. As in the case example of Sam described later in the chapter, one way people can get stuck following a suicide is by taking an excessive amount of personal responsibility and blame for the event. As with Sam, a firefighter who lost a colleague to suicide, this can be affected by an individual's overall guilt proneness (Chapter 20). The case example demonstrates how guilt over a colleague's suicide, and guilt proneness more generally, may be addressed concurrently in therapy.

Two additional common ways patients can get stuck in their processing of a suicide are worth mentioning. Some people bring an analytical approach to trying to make sense of the suicide. However, because suicide is not typically a rational act, the analytical approach is not the right tool to use to understand it. Such individuals struggle immensely to get past the question, "how could they do such a thing?" This can be accompanied by emotions such as bewilderment, confusion, or anger toward the deceased individual.

With patients who struggle this way, I typically start by validating that it is natural to want to understand what would motivate someone to take such a drastic, extreme step of ending their own life. I highlight to the client the cyclical, never-ending nature of exploring "why?" and "how could they do this?" I help them realize that the only person who might be able to answer these questions conclusively is no longer alive. I help them see the questioning of "why?" as a trap and a thought process that contributes to emotional distress without resolution, and thus, that persisting in it is not serving them.

To help patients deliberately exit this questioning loop, I support them in formulating a response to the recurrent question based on what is known. In the event of a suicide, this response may be, "He must have been in enormous pain to end his life this way," as a response to the ever-present "why?" Then, when the recurrent question arises again, patients are guided to remind themselves of the answer they came up with. They are then guided to use in-the-moment mindfulness practice to disengage from the repetitive question and bring attention to their present-moment sensory experience. Over the course of weeks or months, the question "why?" and other repetitive questions begin to occur less frequently when they no longer successfully capture attention and psychological effort. It is worth noting, too, that analysis is a common way of avoiding difficult feelings. The reduction in the focus on answering these questions often makes way for the grief process to unfold more fully, often ultimately leading to integration and acceptance of the loss.

For patients stuck not in questioning but in judgment and anger toward the deceased person, an effort is made instead to shift from judgment to compassion. Even without knowing anything about the person's life, the suicide itself is sufficient evidence of intense pain and suffering. In my view, people who are living satisfying and meaningful lives do not kill themselves. Some patients do struggle with accessing compassion and require other interventions to be able to do so, but most are gradually able to access some degree of sadness, grief, and compassion toward the deceased.

Another group of patients, in my experience, responds in a very different way to completed suicides. These tend to be individuals who have had significant mental health struggles, even suicidality, in their personal histories. These individuals, when faced with a completed suicide, easily identify with the individual who ended their own life. They may become preoccupied with empathy and identification with the deceased, which, in reality, is blended with their own unprocessed pain from their own past struggles. They may also become intensely fearful that they, too, given their histories, will one day harm or kill themselves.

With this type of reaction, the work starts with ensuring that there is no significant current risk of suicide. Provided there is not, the therapy work focuses on helping the client separate their own pain from that of the deceased. It may not be obvious why this would be needed, but in my experience, this is one place where our own unprocessed pain and suffering can become emotionally blended with our perception of the pain of another. After all, we can never truly know the experience of another person directly. Instead, we infer the experiences of others through our own experiences.

Initially, the therapy focus shifts from speaking about the suicide and the deceased to the client's own history of adversity and mental health struggles. Patients often begin to share about scary, painful times filled with helplessness, memories of which have been triggered by the recent suicide. Before they can process the suicide itself, patients may need support in accessing their own emotions about about their own periods of personal struggle, as well as compassion for their former struggling selves.

As the client grieves and learns to access compassion for their former, suffering self, they are also guided to notice and celebrate all the ways that they are no longer that same person. They are helped to reflect on and recognize the growth and healing that has happened between their past adversity and the present, with a focus on meaningful changes which may include fostering healthy, supportive relationships, finding their calling professionally, and their work and progress in therapy that has resulted in healing and growth. Grieving their past pain, celebrating the growth that has taken place since, and affirming their commitment to a life worth living can help separate the parts of the reaction to the suicide that were, in reality, their own pain and suffering triggered by the death of another.

Having done the work described above, the focus can shift to reflecting on, remembering, and grieving for the person who has died by suicide. Patients often spontaneously begin to feel sadness and compassion toward the deceased person, for the suffering this individual endured that led to the suicide. If they had a meaningful relationship with the person who has died, they also grieve their own loss of this person in their lives. Free from the blending of their own story with that of the deceased, the emotional processing of the suicide can proceed more directly, and in due time, the loss can be assimilated and, to some degree, accepted.

CASE EXAMPLE | "I should have seen it coming"

Sam, a late-career firefighter, became tearful in session for the first time as he shared an event from many years ago that had a lasting impact on him. Robert, a member of his platoon, had completed suicide years prior. Although Robert and Sam were not very close, Sam was one of the last people Robert spoke to before leaving work on his final shift. Sam had difficulty shaking the feeling that he should have somehow sensed that something with Robert was "off," thus having maybe had an opportunity to prevent the tragic outcome. As we explored the lasting impact of Robert's suicide, Sam also realized that Robert's death took place just as he was beginning to experience symptoms of depression himself. Robert's suicide forced him to confront the belief that if left unchecked, his depression may one day lead him, too, to attempt suicide. Thus, a work-related exposure to the suicide of a peer triggered Sam's own fears about his own death, something Sam had been avoiding for many years.

Sam's treatment spanned many months and covered many themes. Direct challenging of his sense of responsibility for Robert's death yielded, at best, a modest shift. We then looked into his history, and the possible roots for his tendency to assume responsibility for the actions of others became apparent. His guilt-proneness, which manifested in many areas of his life, prompted an exploration of his childhood. He shared that he grew up with an alcohol-dependent father who died when Sam was in his early 20s. Growing up, Sam always felt somewhat responsible for his father, believing that had he been different in some way, his father would have overcome his addiction or been able to be more loving and supportive in Robert's life, even despite his addiction.

Sam was gradually able to see the parallel between his excessive sense of responsibility for his father's decisions, his inflated sense of responsibility for Robert's suicide, and his tendency to feel overly responsible in other situations. He was able to experience increased self-compassion for his child self, who craved and lacked a father figure, as well as for his present-day self and for Robert's suffering. He acknowledged that he could not have saved Robert, but vowed to check on his colleagues and offer support, so that none of them would feel isolated and suffer alone like Robert had done. He also reaffirmed his own commitment to overcoming his depression and never giving in to suicidal thinking, due to both his desire to build a life worth living and his wish not to cause by his own actions this degree of pain to his colleagues and loved ones.

Key Points

What is one thing you are taking away from reading this chapter?

____

Action Plan

What is an action you can take to better cope when exposed to suicides?

____

CHAPTER 27

Why Must Good People Suffer?

The question of why 'good' people must suffer has perplexed me since I was a child. It is also an issue that I see my first responder and healthcare professional patients struggle with often. Indeed, having a front row seat to the suffering of innocent people, and especially of children, can really upend one's belief in a just world. This section will examine some spiritual and philosophical perspectives that attempt to make sense of the challenging existential question, "Why do bad things happen to good people?" If spiritual perspectives are not an area of interest for you, or if discussion of themes pertaining to spirituality or religion brings up negative emotions for you, you may prefer to skip this chapter.

Without any framework for making sense of why good and innocent people suffer and die, patients understandably struggle to make sense of what they see, and many fall into the pitfall of concluding that it is somehow they themselves who made the undesirable outcome take place. This may restore some sense of order and control over the situation. The implicit logic seems to be "finally, we know why this tragedy happened—I must have somehow caused it!" But this sense of order and control comes at a high cost. The sense of responsibility often creates agonizing feelings of guilt and shame, a deep pain that many first responders and healthcare professionals carry for decades. In my experience, having a framework or spiritual perspective for suffering and death can help make sense of and provide meaning to these tragic situations.

Understanding the purpose of suffering has long been in the domain of the spiritual traditions. Eastern traditions, such as Buddhism and Hinduism, contain a teaching called karma. Karma, in its simplest terms, refers to the cycle of cause-and-effect that exists across many, many lifetimes. While "karma" is often used colloquially as a synonym for "punishment," this is inaccurate. A karmic view of the world suggests that every event in the present is a result of the totality of all other events (and choices) an individual has made across this and many prior lifetimes. The Zen proverb, "Look at how the snow falls, each flake in its appropriate place" (Tolle, 2005), touches on this belief. Interestingly, Christian and Jewish individuals also hold a belief that no event is random, but is rather a part of "God's plan," as summarized in the passage, "There is a time for everything, and a season for every activity under the heavens." (Ecclesiastes 3:2).

It is too easy, when we witness events involving suffering that seem unfair or death that seems premature, to see them as some sort of cosmic error. In a just world, innocent children should not suffer or die. I cannot offer a conclusive answer as to why such tragic things happen, and like you, I wish they never did. But, as a psychologist, I spend many of my days hearing about tragic events in the lives of my patients and in the lives of those they care for and serve. Given that tragic things do happen, I believe that a perspective or framework that provides some way of making sense of tragic events like this, whether due to a higher power such as God, or due to the totality of the events preceding it, such as karma, or any other framework that helps make sense of such events, can be helpful.

I am not suggesting that we must all believe in the Eastern notion of karma, or in the Judeo-Christian notion of "God's plan." A metaphysical view of the world is not a fit for many of us. At the very least, however, I invite you to consider that each and every event, from the drowning of a child to the suicide of a patient or colleague, has numerous proximal and distal causes. It is an oversimplification, in my view, to believe that any event occurs in isolation, and this way of thinking leaves us more vulnerable to attempt to blame either ourselves or someone else. If we are able to perceive that every event, including our own choices and actions, occurs within an interconnected web of causality, we can still do everything within our power and skill to help shape outcomes, but we are far less likely to take complete responsibility for how events play out. Allow me to demonstrate this using a concrete example.

CASE EXAMPLE | Who Is to Blame?

Imagine a mother taking her two children, ages three and six, to the grocery store. After checking out, the young mother rolls her full cart and holds onto her three-year-old's hand toward the parking lot. Her older child merrily skips toward the family car a few yards ahead of mom, delighted to have successfully convinced her mom to get both her favorite snacks and a small toy.

In the parking lot, a woman in her mid-70s is in the process of backing out of a parking spot. She had not slept well for several nights, still processing her husband's recent cancer diagnosis. She does not see the child approaching as she backs out of the parking spot, and begins reversing her car just as the skipping child enters her sight, but it is a moment too late to stop, and the child is hit. Let us say for the sake of the exercise that the woman manages to brake right away, and that the child in this story is mildly injured, remains alive, and recovers fully over the course of the coming weeks.

Who would you see as responsible for the accident? You might be tempted to say that it is the older woman, after all, she was the driver of the car who hit the child. But what about the mother's duty to safeguard her child in a parking lot? And, what about the six-year-old herself, for having casually strolled behind a car despite being taught many times to stay vigilant when around moving cars? Or, how about the father of the injured child, who has been uncharacteristically absent in recent weeks, working overtime, which led the mother to become depleted, exhausted, and perhaps less vigilant than she would typically be? Or, there is also the father's employer, who made the father work many hours of overtime in recent weeks, preventing him from being more present and helpful to his wife?

I could go on and on for a long time, because for every cause, there are many other causes that came before it. This example is meant to demonstrate how any one event is a link in a web of causality, also known as interdependent causality. For first responders and health-care professionals, simply remembering that every event has many, many causes has the advantage of reducing the desire to find a culprit to blame. This reduces the likelihood of becoming preoccupied with one's own actions or inactions and an inflated sense of personal responsibility (or the actions or inactions of another), thereby avoiding one of the most common emotional pitfalls following a painful event.

Key Points

What is one thing you are taking away from reading this chapter?

___

Action Plan

What is one way you can mitigate the habit of assuming inflated responsibility for the outcomes of events?

Making Meaning of Suffering and Death

A second recurring theme emerged in my reading about suffering and death. The message, simple and profound, was that life is difficult and full of suffering for all of us, and that it is a central purpose of our lives not only to learn to tolerate it, but also to find ways to make meaning out of it. You may be thinking that this sounds like a tall order, and you are quite right. Let us, nevertheless, explore this idea further.

In his seminal book, *Man's Search for Meaning*, Dr. Victor Frankl, a holocaust survivor-turned-psychiatrist, detailed his time in a concentration camp. His immense suffering and loss of many of his loved ones did not break his spirit or diminish his will to live. Even in these dire conditions, he recognized that it was within his capacity to find purpose in his suffering. He stated that it was this quest to make meaning that allowed him to survive the suffering. He resolved to maintain his humanity and compassion and to use his experience to benefit others, and he did just that. He used his insights about surviving the concentration camp to develop an existential psychotherapy, Logotherapy, that supports others to find purpose and meaning within their circumstances (Frankl, 1963).

The Stoics, who lived in the Roman Empire approximately 2000 years ago, came to a similar insight. Their writings emphasized the acceptance and meaning-making of life's trials as a central purpose of being alive. Stoic philosopher Seneca, for example, stated, "Fire is the test of gold; adversity of strong men" (Seneca, ca. 65 CE/2004). To suffer with fortitude while remaining committed to one's ethics is one of the central tenets of Stoic teachings. Famous existential philosopher Nietzsche similarly stated the famous expression, "What does not kill me makes me stronger"" (Nietzsche, 1888).

Suffering and the meaning of suffering are so central to Buddhist teachings that this notion is actually referenced within The Noble Truths, one of the very first messages believed to have been asserted by the Buddha after reaching enlightenment. Thich Nhat Hanh, a Buddhist teacher who dedicated his life to writing about Buddhist principles for lay people, dedicated his book *No Mud No Lotus: The Art of Transforming Suffering* to the relationship between suffering, wisdom, and compassion. The central thesis of this wonderful book is that suffering is a necessary ingredient in helping us develop greater compassion and wisdom, first in reference to our own suffering and then toward others we recognize are also suffering. Thich Nhat Hanh emphasized that we actually need suffering in order to grow, like lotus flowers need mud to grow. "Where there is no mud," exclaimed Hanh, "No lotus flowers are possible" (Hanh, 2014). As a brief aside, I have recommended this book to many of my first responder and healthcare professional patients during times of deep suffering. Those who read it invariably appreciated the book and found parts of it comforting. You do not need to be a Buddhist to find solace in Thich Nhat Hanh's writing which emanates compassion and wisdom and invariably touches the hearts and minds of those who read it.

Another anecdote that demonstrates how to turn suffering into meaning comes to mind. I remember, as a young teen with a fascination for human behavior, that I frequently watched the show "America's Most Wanted," which was created and hosted by John Walsh Jr. Many episodes after starting to watch the show, I was shocked to find out how and why the show came about. I learned of the heartbreaking story of John Walsh's son, Adam Walsh, who was kidnapped and tragically killed. I was initially overcome with sadness for what Adam, John, and their family had surely gone through.

Over time, the sadness gave way to respect and admiration for the fact that, despite his personal pain, John Walsh Jr. devoted the rest of his life to advocating for and helping resolve child disappearances. Not only did he manage to survive the tragic, devastating loss of his son, but he turned his immense suffering into a project that is reported to have helped capture many fugitives in the United States. Of course, the lesson here is not that what happened to Adam Walsh is acceptable; I am sure John Walsh and his family were forever changed by this tragedy. When it comes to adversity and trauma, however, there is no need to choose between the pain and growth that may be possible – both very well can, and often do, coexist in the way we, and those we serve, respond to adversity and truamatic experiences.

In the mental health field, a growing body of literature has emerged exploring the ways that adversity fuels growth, known as "posttraumatic growth." Tedeschi and Calhoun (2004) identified the following domains as particularly likely to show growth following adversity: personal strength, relating to others, new possibilities, appreciation of life, and spiritual and existential change. There is, of course, no expectation that we welcome adversity with open arms, wish it on ourselves or anyone else, or seek it out deliberately. There is no need – life is challenging for all beings and we (and those we serve) will all confront adversity in our lives. The invitation is simply to acknowledge that in adversity, there exists an opportunity for meaning-making and tremendous growth.

In my practice, as individuals heal from traumatic experiences, physical illnesses, or losses of other kinds, they often report becoming more compassionate toward both the self and others, the deepening of their relationships, the emergence of strength and coping skills they did not know they had, and the emergence of gratitude for aspects of life previously taken for granted. It is therefore useful to keep in mind the strength and resilience of those we serve in facing their suffering, the common humanity of pain and suffering, and the fact that, like in the cases of Dr. Frankl, John Walsh Jr., and many of us, these painful experiences may give rise to growth that may otherwise not be possible.

There is another observation I would like to share here about the relationship between suffering and wisdom, compassion, and purpose. Having gotten to know the histories of many first responders and healthcare professionals over nearly two decades, I can confidently say that many of us (myself included) have overcome significant adversity, suffering, and pain in our lives. Many of us have been drawn into helper roles, in fact, for this very reason. We know how painful it can be to suffer, and our own suffering moves us to want to help others suffer less. So, when we are confronted by the suffering of others, it is worthwhile to remember how much adversity we ourselves have overcome, and how much adversity our colleagues in the helping professions have collectively overcome. It is worthwhile to reflect on how instrumental this suffering has been in our growth and in galvanizing our compassion and desire to be of service.

Those of us working in mental health are lucky in this respect. While our patients often come to us in immense suffering, which is at times hard to witness, we have the privilege of seeing the growth that is possible through adversity in real time. I recognize that first responders and many healthcare professionals often do not get to be in this privileged position. Nevertheless, I invite you to trust in the resilience of the person in front of you. They may be in immense pain for the brief moment you are in their lives, but it will not be like this forever. Everything in life is impermanent, and pain and suffering are no exception. When you have done everything you can to alleviate suffering, take solace in the possibility that, like Dr. Victor Frankl, John Walsh Jr., and many of us wounded healers, helpers, and protectors, this very pain may be transformed into growth, compassion, and the inspiration to bring care and kindness into the world.

Moral Injury: A New Frontier in the Understanding of Work-Related Trauma

Moral injury is a relatively new term in the field of traumatic stress. It refers to the psychological, biological, social, behavioral, and spiritual harm that can occur when a person is exposed to events that conflict with their deeply held moral beliefs, values, or ethical codes. These events may involve perpetration, witnessing, failing to prevent, or being betrayed by authority figures or institutions (Litz & Walker, 2025). First responders, healthcare workers, and military personnel are especially vulnerable to moral injuries because our actions on the job can have life-or-death consequences, are often made under time pressure, and are shaped not only by us but also in conjunction with authority figures and organizational policies.

In my experience witnessing and treating moral injury in healthcare professionals and first responders, morally injurious events vary but their impacts are commonly one of the following: (1) a feeling of self-blame, shame, and self-criticism for actions taken by oneself, that violate deeply held morals and ethics held by the individual, or (2) a feeling of having been betrayed by a person, especially in a position of power, or by a group or organization that was previously trusted. In both cases, there is a feeling of enormous dissonance and upset, as actions or omissions violate deeply held beliefs, ethics, and expectations.

CASE EXAMPLE | Moral Injury During the COVID-19 Pandemic

Several years ago, humanity experienced an enormous collective challenge during the COVID-19 pandemic. Those working in first responder and healthcare roles were truly at the forefront as we collectively tried to contain and confront this unprecedented wave of illness and death. During this difficult period, a number of situations contributed to moral injury among many professionals working on the frontlines.

One morally injurious event discussed in the context of the pandemic is the reality that, due to hospitals being overwhelmed with large numbers of patients, hospital staff had to ration medicine, beds, and medical equipment. This resulted in staff being forced to make heartbreaking choices about who would receive access to the limited medical resources, potentially contributing to morbidity and even deaths in some patients. This type of experience can create enormous moral distress, including feelings of personal transgression and guilt, as well as a sense of betrayal by the system for having been put in this position (Hines et al., 2021).

Another morally injurious situation associated with the pandemic was the inability to allow loved ones into the hospital room of patients due to fears of spreading the virus. As a result of this, severely ill COVID-19 patients, many of whom succumbed to the virus, spent their final hours alone, isolated from loved ones. Having to enforce this precaution, in the name of reducing spread, violated the deeply held value in medicine of allowing dying patients to derive comfort from the presence of their loved ones, and watching these individuals suffer in isolation contributed to moral injury among the medical staff (Sudai, 2021).

Our understanding of moral injury, how it contributes to and is distinct from related syndromes such as post-traumatic stress disorder (PTSD) and depression, is emerging. From what is known at this time, here are a few recommendations for overcoming moral injury (based, in part, on Litz & Walker, 2025).

- **Disclosure to trusted others can be a powerful antidote to guilt and shame.** There is a popular saying in psychology, "shame thrives in darkness." I have seen firsthand the impact of sharing in therapy groups or among colleagues, where our peers can validate and normalize our experiences and responses to events. This also opens the door to hearing and integrating alternate, more validating, views on your actions than the self-critical views that may initially emerge.
- **Commit to and engage in any available repair**. Take deliberate action congruent with the ethics and morals that have been challenged by the morally injurious experience. Express remorse and seek forgive-

ness if possible, engage in volunteerism, donate to organizations, and advocate for changes that would help others.

- **Commit to learning and growth through the painful experience**. When the past action cannot be undone, and repair is not possible, the best we can do is commit to acting differently in the future. Ask yourself – how can I grow from this experience? Try to commit to specific behaviors informed by this experience.

If the moral injury involves a sense of betrayal by another person, group, or organization, consider the following recommendations:

- **Consider joining groups that share similar ethics and values.** Find opportunities to be with others who engage in compassionate, trustworthy, selfless, and humane ways. As much as possible, find opportunities to be with others who share and act according to the ethics and values that are important to you.
- **Consider the various causes for the injurious event.** If possible, advocate for change, educate others, or take whatever action is possible to prevent a similar event in the future. Consider also whether viable alternatives were or were not available at the time the morally injurious choices were selected, as sometimes suboptimal choices are made in the absence of alternatives.
- **Consider the likelihood of similar events taking place in the future.** Sometimes it is possible to shift perspective and build tolerance or forgiveness for violations, and at other times, our moral injury may provide an impetus for change. Trusted others and mental health professionals may be able to help identify ways to protect yourself from future events leading to moral injury.

Key Points

What is one thing you are taking away from reading this chapter?

___

Action Plan

What is one action you can take to recover from or prevent experiences of moral injury?

___

CHAPTER 28

Finding Meaning In Our Work

Many patients have shared that they chose careers in healthcare and first responder roles for the opportunity to make a difference in the lives of others. Yet, many of us find ourselves gradually depleted by years of training, overwhelmed by ever-growing caseloads, and feeling limited in the kind of help we can offer. With these challenges, it is easy to become cynical, frustrated by systemic barriers and challenges, and to lose touch with the meaningful parts of our work. However, it is still possible to find meaning in our roles by being mindful of how much our actions can impact others, even unintentionally, as well as by seeking additional opportunities to make a positive impact on others.

Dr. Irvin Yalom, an American psychiatrist and author practicing existential psychotherapy, introduced the term "rippling," a term he coined for our capacity to make a difference in the lives of others. Dr. Yalom describes rippling as follows:

> I think we ripple on into others, just like a stone puts its ripples into a brook. That, for me too, is a source of comfort. It kind of, in a sense, negates the sense of total oblivion. Some piece of ourselves, not necessarily our consciousness, but some piece of ourselves gets passed on and on and on. Specifically, it is our actions toward others that have a lasting impact on those around us, even when we ourselves are gone (Yalom 2008).

For Dr. Yalom, the insight of rippling emerged from his awareness of old age and the approach of death. As we age, it is normal to feel more aware of and unsettled by the fact that our lives and careers are coming to an end. But regardless of whether or not we are currently facing mortality, it is worthwhile to reflect on how we might already be creating positive ripples without recognizing it, as well as finding ways to feel that our daily effort in our work is truly making some positive impact on those around us.

In healthcare and first responder roles, we hold immense power to impact the lives of others in each and every exchange. Through a check-in call to a colleague who hasn't seemed quite like themselves recently, a well-timed intervention with a patient, or a genuine expression of gratitude to the support staff of the hospital or emergency service, we can exert an enormous impact on someone else, truly helping them feel seen, validated, and appreciated.

Often, due to the busy and stressful lives that we lead, we can lose sight of the power we hold to impact others through our words and deeds. And sometimes, our words and actions can cause unintended harm. I will share a brief personal anecdote to illustrate this notion.

About a decade ago, in my mid-20s, I became a mom to twins. The pregnancy was riddled with complications, the babies were born prematurely, and we all contracted a serious blood infection at the time of birth, which we luckily overcame. Needless to say, this chain of events took an enormous physical and emotional toll, and recovery took some time.

When my sons were about six months of age, during the cold Canadian winter, they contracted respiratory syncytial virus (RSV). This virus is usually mild, except in infants, for whom it is often deadly. One of my sons appeared to be having some respiratory distress, and, frightened by the prospect of losing him after all we have been through, we called for emergency services. By the time paramedics arrived, his breathing and color had improved. Seeing a seemingly stable, breathing baby with what appeared to be a simple cold, one of the paramedics implied sarcastically and not-so-subtly that we should not have wasted his time. He and his partner completed all the appropriate medical checks and left. But his cold, dismissive demeanor left us with feelings of embarrassment and shame for having called for emergency services.

It has been almost thirteen years since this took place, and I am grateful to say that my son recovered fully and is now a healthy and thriving teen. Yet, I remember the exchange and especially the sting of the paramedic's judgment with surprising clarity. I share this not to shame anyone – I, too, have said things in moments of frustration or exhaustion that I wish I could take back. I recognize that the work of first responders can be incredibly depleting, resulting in good people not always showing up at their best. I share this story as a cautionary tale to illustrate just how amplified the impact of our words and actions, whether good or bad, can be when a person is already vulnerable and in distress. I encourage each of us to try to be mindful of the ripples we create, moment by moment. Let us, as much as possible, use our words and deeds to heal rather than to inflict pain.

I often witness with pride that, through the course of therapy, patients begin to feel more accepting and loving within themselves, and their desire to make a positive difference in the lives of others often returns or grows. When we ourselves are hurting, it may be hard to feel a strong desire to help others, as our system knows intuitively that we must first focus on supporting ourselves. If you are struggling to find your desire to impact others positively, it may be that at this moment, you need to turn your attention inward, toward your own healing and care. It could also, of course, mean that some external change, such as a change in role or work situation, may be needed. Trusted peers, friends, and therapists can help guide us back to finding our work meaningful and fulfilling. I encourage you to explore ways to derive more meaning from your work. We spend about half of our lives working, and finding our work meaningful is protective for our mental health and motivating for our desire to continue to serve.

Here are some recommendations to reflect on in order to maximize the sense of meaning and purpose in your professional pursuits.

- **Try to recall what drew you to your chosen vocation.** Consider to what degree you continue to engage with the aspects of your profession that drew you to it and that you genuinely enjoy and find meaningful.
- **Recognize that small gestures can make a big difference**. Making a positive difference in the lives of those around you is not only in the heroics of rescue or the skilled delivery of your professional role. It is also in the small daily actions – asking a colleague how they're really doing and taking the time to listen, offering small gestures of support, and offering gratitude for tasks that are often taken for granted. Is it possible for you to increase your impact on others by focusing on these seemingly small and accessible acts?
- **Do not discount the ripples you are already making.** Many first responders and healthcare professionals tend to discount the times they have done their job very well, or made someone (a patient, colleague, or friend) feel seen and valued. Are there actions you already take but do not dwell on? I encourage you to focus on these successes, praise yourself, and fully accept praise from others without downplaying or discounting it.
- **Reflect on ways to make your workdays feel more meaningful**. Ask yourself whether there are specific tasks and roles that you find especially meaningful. What is it about them that makes it so satisfy-

ing for you, and are there ways to seek out opportunities to have these experiences?

- **Ask yourself what changes you might need to make, personally or professionally, to feel a greater sense of purpose.** For many practitioners, changes can be made within their current job and career to enhance their sense of meaning and purpose. For others, more dramatic changes (of place of work or job role) need to be considered. If you are truly struggling to find a sense of purpose and meaning in your current role, reflect on how important it is for you to have this in your professional life. If this feels important, consider what options may be available to you to allow you to once again take pride in your work, and what the costs of making these changes might be.

Key Points

What is one thing you are taking away from reading this chapter?

____

Action Plan

What is one action you can take to cultivate greater purpose and meaning in your work?

____

CHAPTER 29

Cultivating Pleasure, Gratitude, and Connection

Much of what has been shared so far in this book pertains to mental and emotional distress, painful feelings, and challenges that may arise in conjunction with first responder and healthcare work. This section will focus on the other side of the equation – the lifestyle habits of those who manage to lead balanced, fulfilling, joy-filled lives and who balance caring for themselves and others well.

Over the years, I have had the pleasure of supporting a number of incredibly high-functioning, highly resilient patients who thrive in their challenging professional roles and in their personal lives. They have shown me that it is possible, though not easy, to stay well while in the service of others. In working with these individuals, I have started to observe some patterns in their traits and habits that appear to help them weather the challenges and adversities of first responder and healthcare roles. Here are some characteristics of helpers who thrive:

1. **They appreciate and prioritize relaxation and rest.** First responders and healthcare professionals who thrive know what is restful and restorative for them, and are unapologetically disciplined in finding regular opportunities for these activities even while holding busy professional roles.

2. **They surround themselves with people and situations that are nourishing rather than depleting to them.** They cultivate close friendships with people who are supportive and encouraging, but let go of relationships that are harmful. They engage in regular exercise, hobbies, and other pursuits that offer pleasure, distraction, and novelty and adventure to offset the stressors of their work.

3. **They cultivate a support system at work and outside of it**. They have people they can talk to about their work experiences, but they

also spend time with people outside their profession, with whom they can let go of their work persona and just be themselves.

4. **They are attuned with their bodies and emotions and take their health seriously**. They have focused on cultivating self-compassion (in place of self-criticism) either naturally or through healing in therapy. They do not overidentify with the savior or rescuer role toward those they serve. Instead, they are humbly aware that while their role is to help, they do not have control over all the outcomes. They take pride in the times they were able to help and do not punish themselves for the times their efforts did not yield the results they had hoped for.
5. **They cultivate spirituality and reflect on, rather than avoid, difficult topics such as suffering and death.** They have reflected on the major questions in life, including issues of purpose, suffering, and death. They have made sense of these for themselves, sometimes through organized religion, but often through a more personal, flexible approach to spirituality. They have accepted death and impermanence and prioritize cultivating both pleasure and meaning in life.
6. **They practice their respective professions with a deep sense of purpose**. They are connected with a desire to be of service and ease the suffering of others. They are realistic, however, in knowing and accepting that they may be limited in what they can do for a given person, and they do not take on more responsibility for events than is theirs.
7. **They are unafraid to make changes**. Well, that is not entirely accurate. Often, the healthiest individuals are understandably afraid of leaving the known for the unknown. This may be a role, workplace, or a long-term relationship. But, in my observation, individuals who thrive do not stay indefinitely in situations (roles, workplaces, or relationships) that do not serve them and which have shown themselves to not be amenable to change. Individuals who thrive are unafraid to work to make situations better, but leave if this does not work, as they value and prioritize their own well-being above comfort or security.

Presence and Gratitude

Our minds evolved to keep us safe, and for this goal, recognizing the threatening elements of experience is more relevant to our survival than the positive ones. From the strict standpoint of survival, it is in the mind's interest to remember the negative attributes of a situation to try and avoid the threat or negative consequence in the future. As a result of this bias, our mind naturally orients toward and focuses on threatening stimuli rather than on positive or neutral aspects of life (Blanchette, 2006). This is perhaps especially true when we work in occupations where there is stress, pressure, and danger. Thus, finding places, activities, and people that allow for safety and positive emotions is an important practice for maintaining psychological well-being.

Thich Nhat Hanh wrote extensively about mindfulness, and his writings stand out for distilling its philosophy in a clear and accessible way. He often spoke about the importance of being able to generate feelings of happiness by bringing attention to the sources of happiness that are already present right now. This is radically different than the typical way in which most of us go through our lives, either stressed by the difficulties of the present moment or waiting for the next thing to happen before we can slow down, relax, and take in the good elements of life. The practice of turning toward the good serves as an entry point to the feeling of gratitude (Hanh, 2009).

The wise practice of focusing on the positive aspects of experience sounds simple, but over time, it can profoundly shape our experience of reality. This turning of the mind toward the good is echoed by neuroscientist Dr. Rick Hanson in his book *Hardwiring Happiness*. He explains that positive experiences are far less "sticky" in our mind than are threatening ones, for the evolutionary reason described earlier. To spend more of our time in states of ease, happiness, and gratitude, we must therefore practice turning toward and "taking in the good" in our lives when conditions of calm, safety, and happiness are present (Hanson, 2013).

Reminding ourselves of the transient, impermanent nature of all things can, in my experience, make it much easier to access feelings of joy and gratitude in the present. For example, I have personally found it beneficial to remind myself, when looking at my children or a beautiful bloom in the spring, that both are only here for a short period of time— my kids will soon be grown and no longer little, and the spring beauty will fade. This is, for me at least, a nudge to get out of my mind (and off of my phone) to truly engage with what is here in the present. I invite you to practice taking in the good, using this strategy or any other that works for you. This mindset could have helped me put my worries aside and enjoy my precious time on my trip to Italy, rather than missing potential moments of happiness and gratitude, as I will describe shortly.

The relationship between gratitude and impermanence is illustrated in the following story, attributed to spiritual teacher Ajahn Chah, as reported by his disciple and Buddhist teacher and author Dr. Jack Kornfield.

"For me this glass is already broken. I enjoy it; I drink out of it. It holds my water admirably, sometimes even reflecting the sun in beautiful patterns. If I should tap it, it has a lovely ring to it. But when I put this glass on the shelf and the wind knocks it over or my elbow brushes it off the table and it falls to the ground and shatters, I say, 'of course'. When I understand that the glass is already broken, every moment with it is precious" (Kornfield, 2008).

It is undeniable that all things, good and bad, are impermanent. They don't stay the same. Your toddler will grow, your cup of coffee will become cold or empty, the fragrant lilac will wilt, and unfortunately, you and your loved ones will part. This is not meant to sound morbid or distressing; it is simply a reminder to practice turning away from the habitual focus on threat and toward being radically present. When something wonderful happens, or when there is a simple moment of ease, pleasure, or connection, let us train ourselves to truly savor it.

CASE EXAMPLE | Forgotten Trip To Italy

Before I discovered mindfulness and learned to shift my mind toward the present moment, like many of my patients, I was very prone to worry. One event really stands out in my mind, showing the high cost of not being present. While I was a graduate student, my husband and I took a once-in-a-lifetime trip across Italy, a place I had dreamed of visiting. I remember, somewhat comically but with regret, that as I walked down the beautiful streets of Rome, Venice, and Florence, I was hardly able to perceive my surroundings. I was so preoccupied with my research proposal and getting through my demanding graduate program. Because this was on my mind for most of the trip, I have almost no memory of its sights and experiences. I was in Italy physically, but not mentally or emotionally.

If I could turn back time, I would go back to the trip in Italy and savor every moment – fully take in all the incredible sights, take time to taste and enjoy the delicious food and coffee, dance and sing along with the music, and immerse myself in interactions with local people. This is the practice of mindfulness, fully experiencing moments of safety and abundance —a simple yet life-changing practice. In your day-to-day life, when enjoying a quiet cup of coffee, walking down a trail, smelling a fragrant flower, listening to the laughter of your child, or holding the hand of your loved one, bring attention to the sensations and feelings, and acknowledge that this is a moment full of joy, pleasure, and peace.

Perhaps, had I recognized the impermanence of my brief opportunity to enjoy Italy, I would have savored every moment of it and let go of my worries for some time. Practice letting go of your worries, even for a moment, to fully experience the present moment, and this can become a habit. To shift into the present moment, savor everyday experiences (and special ones) all the while remembering (and learning to accept) that all of life is impermanent. This set of insights and practices makes it easier to have a rich and satisfying life without actually having to change the circumstances of your day-to-day experience, but rather, by shifting the focus of your attention while you are experiencing them.

While the discussion thus far focused on gratitude for our own life experiences, gratitude is also powerful when authentically directed toward others, especially when used to notice strengths and appreciate the presence and contributions of those around you. Expressing and receiving gratitude bears great significance in the lives of first responders and healthcare professionals, and we can all contribute through our actions to maximizing the presence of gratitude at our workplaces. The following example illustrates this.

CASE EXAMPLE | The Gift of Gratitude

Judith was an experienced nurse in her 50s, working for many years in labor and delivery. She has shared considerable frustration that, as one of the most seasoned nurses on the unit, her colleagues and management expected so much from her, particularly in ongoing mentorship of the unit's many new hires, alongside her own heavy workload. She managed to cope with this for some time, but it has gotten especially challenging to keep up, as she began experiencing symptoms of menopause while also caring for her ailing mother when not at work.

She shared that she often left work feeling unseen and unappreciated. She had been considering leaving her current role because she was unsure how much longer she would be able to keep up.

Judith shared that on a day when she was feeling especially depleted, one of the staff physicians came up to her and thanked her for her skillful handling of a number of challenging situations over the past few weeks. As she shared this, her demeanor brightened and her eyes became moist with tears. In this brief encounter, she shared that she felt seen and appreciated in a deep and meaningful way, something she had not felt for some time. While the overarching questions about her professional future still remained, this encounter gave her the strength and motivation to keep serving in her current role a while longer.

When we feel tired, depleted, or stressed, we tend to engage in negative thinking, judgment, and fault-finding not only toward ourselves but also toward those around us. In this way, stress can be contagious within teams, as one person's stress can create stress for those around them. Yet, we all likely know how meaningful it is to feel seen, have our work and efforts validated and appreciated, and how hurtful it feels to be subjected to criticism or to be taken for granted.

As we learn to turn deliberately toward the good in our own lives, let us also begin to practice noticing and acknowledging our peers and mentors, both in how they fulfill their duties and in how they support their colleagues and peers in the helping and service professions. A word of validation, when genuine and well-timed, is easy to give and can have an enormous positive impact on each of us, especially as most of us are far too hard on ourselves.

Cultivating Social Connection Within and Outside of the Profession

Many patients finally seek therapy when their most trusted colleagues express worries about their well-being. Service-related cumulative stress tend to happen gradually, and an individual may be less aware of the subtle changes in them than those closest to them. I encourage my patients, whenever possible, to try and find peers they can trust and open up to, and to invest in nurturing these relationships. Supportive peers can be an enormous asset to psychological wellness in the following ways:

1. **Peers really get what it's like to do the job, both day-to-day and on the worst days.** After a particularly challenging emergency call or hospital shift, a colleague can offer validation and heartfelt empathy for your difficult experiences and resulting reactions, as they have likely faced similar situations themselves. Many professionals fear burdening or traumatizing family members and friends with shocking details of emergency calls, fatalities in the hospital setting, and other emotionally impactful work-related situations they face at work. The space created among peers where we can speak in an unfiltered way, gore and all, and receive empathy and validation can truly be invaluable. It also serves important therapeutic functions in helping emotional processing following a difficult event.
2. **Peers are often the first to notice that you're struggling.** For many of my patients, comments by trusted colleagues were the triggers for them to recognize that they were not doing well and to initiate therapy. Supportive peers keep an eye on each other, check in, and express concern when a colleague seems to be struggling. For this reason, I believe that peers in the profession are the first line of defense for each of us in managing and protecting our mental health.
3. **Peers may be aware of resources that may be available.** You might be surprised how many of your peers may be going to therapy, have tried medications, or have accessed other resources that may be available to individuals within your profession, both from within the organization and outside of it. They may be able to recommend therapists and other providers that they have found helpful in the past. They may have also developed certain "hacks" for coping with specific challenges in a given workplace (e.g., where to most easily find a microwave while working on the road) that could make your workday go by more smoothly.
4. **Peers can normalize the expression of vulnerability and the act of seeking supports.** Organizations are going to great lengths to encourage their members to seek mental health supports when needed. Yet, there is still considerable stigma related to having mental health challenges and seeking help. Many of us carry internalized

> stigma and shame for this, as well. To be told by a respected peer or mentor that they, too, have struggled, have gone to therapy, and have found ways to thrive, is one of the most powerful ways we can support peers and new recruits in the profession. It may give a struggling peer, especially a junior colleague, a sense of being normal as well as much needed hope for recovery.
>
> As a mental health clinician, I am confident that the stigma surrounding admitting to struggling with mental health and shame for seeking help continues to claim the lives of first responders and health-care professionals. I encourage my own patients to reflect on what they can personally do to fight the stigma. This includes continuing to seek help when needed and being mindful of their interactions with peers in the profession. The degree of disclosure is an individual decision, and only you can decide how much to share and with whom. But for many of my patients, the act of sharing their experiences of healing and, in doing so, supporting colleagues in their dark times has been a meaningful and highly rewarding choice.

So, as you make choices about where and with whom to work, try to prioritize being in a supportive, collegial environment free of unnecessary drama. This will allow you to conserve your psychological and physical resources for work, family, and your own well-being. And, if trusted peers express concerns about changes they see in you, try to really take their words in. Feedback from people you trust can be a valuable source of information about your mental health and an impetus to seek necessary support.

Practice Exercise: Pleasant Activity Planning

Take a moment to consider whether there are any activities that help you relax or bring you pleasure. When was the last time you engaged in this activity? Have you made relaxation and enjoyment a priority in your life? Pick an activity from the list below to engage in once per week for the coming weeks and observe the impact of this on your physical and mental well-being. To make the practice even more effective, consider bringing mindful attention and gratitude to the activity you select.

- Yoga
- Martial arts
- Dance

- Attending religious or spiritual gatherings
- Gardening
- Meditation or mindfulness practice
- Swimming
- Walking in nature
- Staying in a nature cabin or cottage
- Growing plants indoors
- Cuddling a cat or dog
- Jogging
- Spin class
- Working out
- Painting, sculpting or other crafts
- Listening to or playing music
- Journaling
- Reading or listening to audiobooks
- Spending time with extended family
- Going to the movies or seeing a play
- Playing board games
- Going on a date
- Spending time with friends
- Trying a new restaurant
- Traveling to new places
- Playing video games
- Spending time with colleagues outside of work

Key Points

What is one thing you are taking away from reading this chapter?

____

Action Plan

What is one thing you can do to cultivate pleasure, gratitude, presence, and connection?

____

CHAPTER 30

Mental Health Stigma and De-Mystifying Therapy

First responder and healthcare organizations have come a long way in protecting the mental health of employees. These days, I often hear of supervisors and leaders taking the time to check on the well-being of staff members and offering understanding, compassion, and practical support when an employee is struggling. The efforts to highlight the importance of mental health seem to be making a significant difference. More than ever, early-career first responders and healthcare professionals are proactively seeking psychological services while they are well, rather than waiting for stressors or psychological distress to arise. While these changes are worthy of pride and celebration, there is still a need for all of us to contribute, individually and collectively, to the de-stigmatization of experiencing and disclosing emotional struggles and the act of going for therapy.

The pressure to avoid emotional vulnerability appears to be particularly strong for males, and for those working in work cultures that emphasize machismo and traditional definitions of masculinity, such as policing, fire services, surgical and emergency medicine, and in military environments. The pressure to appear emotionally unfazed by events, unfortunately, is not without mental health costs, as the natural expression of emotions is frequently suppressed or otherwise avoided in such settings.

If you work in a setting that penalizes speaking about and displaying emotions, you are not alone. Do consider finding places and people — whether colleagues, friends, or professional supports —with whom you can regularly feel safe enough to tune inward, feel, acknowledge, and express the emotions arising within you, facilitating their processing.

I encourage you to take a moment now to reflect on the question, "Who are the people with whom I feel safest to acknowledge, feel, and express emotions?" This may be a peer, peer support at work, spouse or family member, a spiritual leader, or a therapist. It does not have to be at the workplace, a place where many feel pressured to present a calm, unaffected emotional exterior. It also does not have to be at the exact moment when the emotion arises.

I have many first responders and healthcare professional patients who meet with me once a month or every second month, even though they are generally functioning very well and are not currently distressed. I find that, before long, a difficult patient situation, tense interaction with a colleague, or triggering emergency call arises. Because of the established therapeutic relationship, we can dive right in and begin to work through the experience and obtain relief without delay. My message here is that it is not necessary to wait for distress to arise – just as we make time for a dental cleaning to keep our teeth healthy, rather than waiting for a cavity to form, we should also make time for regular mental health check-ins and skills learning opportunities as a form of prevention against psychological distress.

All of us can contribute in some way to reducing the mental health stigma in our workplaces. Here are a few points to consider in reflecting on what we can each do toward our shared goal of reducing mental health stigma in our healthcare and first responder workplaces:

- **Fighting stigma is our shared responsibility.** Consider whether you may benefit from therapy or access to mental health content. Even those of us who function well can still learn and grow psychologically and emotionally. Consider whether you may have some internalized mental health stigma, such as a belief that only "broken" people go to therapy. If you are not doing so already, try to read books on mental health topics, occasionally listen to content related to areas of emotional functioning that interest you, and seek therapy for either treatment or prevention purposes.
- **Find a few colleagues with whom you feel safe enough to be vulnerable.** Make a point of checking in with each other regularly, and be mindful not to penalize disclosure with judgment. When you are in your professional role, there may not be time to attend to your inner terrain, your own thoughts and emotions in depth. In those moments, I still encourage my patients to notice how a situation makes them feel, perhaps with a simple, "Ouch, it is so sad to be seeing this right now." Commit to yourself to come back to process this experience further, and come back to it, alone or with support, as soon as it is feasible to do so.

- **If you are a supervisor or in a leadership role, try to model healthy expression of emotions with your peers and subordinates.** This does not mean displaying intense, uncontrolled emotions. But a simple acknowledgment, like saying, "Wow, that pediatric code was so sad," or even shedding a tear during particularly painful situations, gives permission to those who report to you to be authentic with their emotions.
- **Be mindful of what you say and the jokes you make.** I hesitate to raise this issue, as I can appreciate that humor is an important and helpful way for first responders and healthcare professionals to discharge stress and build a sense of community. I have also heard of cases where humor has been used to make fun of someone who had made a mistake, stumbled during a critical moment, showed vulnerability, cried, or took time off work for mental health reasons. This could involve making fun of a peer, but also of a patient or family member in their absence. Please be very mindful that when you make jokes or use humor, it is not done in a way that could add shame and distress to someone who may already be in a difficult place. While all colleagues around you may be smiling and laughing along in the moment, there is a fair chance that at least some of them are struggling psychologically in some way. Use humor often—it is a great tool for coping and building community— but be cautious when making jokes at the expense of others, which may inadvertently wound someone who may be listening.
- **If you have benefited from mental health services, taken time off work due to stress, or found helpful mental health resources, consider sharing generously.** Disclosure is a personal choice, and if it is not for you, that is totally valid. At the same time, junior first responders, nurses, and physicians have shared with me that when senior, respected, and admired colleagues disclosed past struggles, this was validating, helpful, and de-stigmatizing. Indeed, finding out that someone you look up to at work has struggled, gone off work, or gone to therapy goes a long way in reducing shame and gives permission for others to consider the same. Depending on your role, seniority, and willingness to share, consider whether this is a way you may be able to "ripple" positively and meaningfully impact those around you.

- **Be mindful of your reactions when a colleague discloses mental health struggles or takes time off from work.** Quite a number of my patients over the years have recalled with pain hearing their respected colleagues mutter that a peer is "milking the system." Others have been hurt by hearing peers judging a colleague for going on stress leave, insinuating that they are not suited for the job. It is not hard to imagine how colleagues who are struggling may be hurt and shamed by hearing such talk. So, when someone discloses struggle, seeks referrals for therapists, or takes time off work, try to give them the benefit of the doubt that their pain is real, and offer support and compassion, or at least do not judge or doubt them. While there are likely a few individuals who inflate and over-report symptoms, I have generally found that first responders and healthcare professionals far more frequently downplay and minimize distress, as opposed to exaggerating it. So, if a peer is saying that they are struggling emotionally, believe them and support them to the best extent you can, or at least do not add to their suffering. Peers are the first line of psychological defense for first responders and healthcare professionals, and the consequences of invalidation and judgment of a vulnerable colleague by trusted peers, in my view, can be truly catastrophic.

CASE EXAMPLE | "Toxic Masculinity"

Max, a junior police officer, came to therapy after beginning to develop PTSD symptoms following a call involving a young man's suicide. Seeing a man of his own age who had ended his life by suicide was painful and heartbreaking for him, especially as he had struggled with depression and suicidality in his teens. While responding to the call, he was surprised to see the other first responders on scene, apparently unfazed, making jokes about the young man's home. The seemingly nonchalant reactions of the other responders caused Max to feel shame for experiencing strong emotions, especially since he is now a police officer and believes he is expected to remain calm in any situation. He shared that, among his peers, those who can remain unfazed and "stoic" during difficult calls are regarded as emotionally tough, while those who show negative emotions, such as fear or sadness, are regarded as "weak" and less masculine. Max managed to get through the remainder of the call until he could find a moment of privacy, where he couldn't hold his sadness in anymore and began to cry.

In therapy, Max was shocked to hear me say that his ability to cry is not something to be ashamed of, but something to hold onto, as it means he remains connected to his emotions. He was also guided to notice that he was able to feel his emotions as they arose and still completed all aspects of the call that were required of him skillfully. He learned that through mindfulness strategies, such as deep breathing and bringing mindfulness to his senses in the present moment (sometimes called "grounding"), he could bring the intensity of his emotional arousal down during a stressful call. He was encouraged, however, to make time and space to fully feel and express his emotions to his trusted colleagues, wife, or a therapist. Most of all, he gradually learned that, when acknowledged and expressed in a mindful manner and at an appropriate time, his access to emotions will make him a better, not lesser, cop.

Are You Ready for Therapy?

I sincerely hope that for many of you, reading this book will inspire curiosity and willingness to initiate your own personal psychotherapy, now or in the future. Whether or not you struggle with mental health symptoms right now, first responder and healthcare work is incredibly challenging. It is always possible that the next shift will throw a new challenge at your mental health, and it is my belief that having a mental health professional who knows you and who is ready to help you process a challenging event is a worthwhile time investment best made ahead of any major stressor.

Let us face it—we all have things we can benefit from help with processing, including work stressors, relationship difficulties, past adversity and a multitude of other experiences. It is my hope that what I have shared in this book has helped you identify some areas of psychological work you can do and skills that may need to be strengthened. These are topics worthy of further exploration in individual therapy, and an experienced clinician can deepen your understanding and application of what has been shared here.

Not everyone reading this book will be ready to pursue therapy, but I hope some readers will be. For this reason, I would like to offer some information on therapy approaches and pose some questions for you to reflect on when it comes time to find a therapist who fits your needs.

Cognitive Behavioral Therapy (CBT)

Cognitive Behavioral Therapy (CBT) is a structured, goal-oriented form of psychotherapy that focuses on the interplay between thoughts, feelings, and behaviors. It operates on the premise that negative thought patterns can lead to emotional distress and maladaptive behaviors. In CBT, individuals are guided to identify and challenge these distorted thoughts, replacing them with more realistic and constructive beliefs. Through various techniques, patients learn to develop healthier coping strategies, ultimately leading to improved emotional regulation and behavioral outcomes. The effectiveness of CBT has been well-documented in treating a range of mental health issues, making it a widely utilized therapeutic approach.

Emotion Focused Therapy (EFT)

Emotion-focused therapy (EFT) centers on helping individuals understand and process their emotions to promote healing and personal growth. This therapeutic approach posits that emotions are key to self-identity and interpersonal relationships. EFT encourages patients to explore their emotional experiences, validate their feelings, and learn how to express them constructively. By fostering emotional awareness, individuals can better navigate their emotional responses, improve their relationships, and cultivate resilience in the face of life's challenges. The goal is to help patients harness their emotional experiences as a means of achieving deeper insight, self-acceptance, and connection with others.

Dialectical Behavior Therapy (DBT)

Dialectical Behavior Therapy (DBT) is a treatment approach that combines standard cognitive-behavioral techniques with mindfulness practices, emphasizing the importance of accepting one's thoughts and feelings while simultaneously working toward change. The therapy focuses on four key areas: mindfulness, distress tolerance, emotion regulation, and interpersonal effectiveness. By teaching patients effective coping strategies and helping them develop healthier relationships, DBT aims to enhance emotional resilience, reduce self-destructive behaviors, and improve overall quality of life.

Acceptance and Commitment Therapy (ACT)

Acceptance and Commitment Therapy (ACT) is a form of psychotherapy that helps individuals live more meaningful and fulfilling lives by teaching them to accept what is out of their personal control and commit to actions that align with their values. Rather than trying to eliminate difficult thoughts and feelings, ACT encourages people to notice, accept, and detach from them—making space for discomfort while moving forward in ways that matter to them. The core goal is to build psychological flexibility, which means being present, open, and able to take effective action, even in the face of pain.

Internal Family Systems (IFS)

Internal Family Systems (IFS) is a therapeutic approach that views the mind as made up of distinct "parts," each with its own perspectives, emotions, and roles. IFS helps patients identify and relate to these internal parts—protectors and exiles—without judgment. Traumatized parts of the mind often hold painful memories or emotions, and protective parts work to keep these buried. The goal of IFS, heavily influenced by Buddhist philosophy, is to access the core Self —a compassionate and centered inner presence that can help heal wounded parts and restore internal harmony. This approach fosters self-understanding and emotional healing by encouraging dialogue between parts and the Self, making it particularly effective for complex trauma and individuals struggling with inner conflict.

Prolonged Exposure (PE)

Prolonged Exposure (PE) is a structured, cognitive-behavioral therapy designed to treat post-traumatic stress disorder (PTSD). PE helps individuals gradually confront trauma-related memories, feelings, and situations that they have been avoiding due to fear or distress. The approach involves two main components: imaginal exposure, where the client repeatedly revisits and recounts the traumatic memory in detail during therapy sessions, and in vivo exposure, where the client gradually approaches safe, real-life situations they have been avoiding because they have served as reminders (or triggers) of the traumatic experience(s). By repeatedly confronting these triggers in a controlled manner and supportive environment, PE reduces the emotional power of the trauma, helping patients process the experience, decrease avoidance behaviors, and regain a sense of control and safety in their lives.

Eye Movement Desensitization and Reprocessing (EMDR)

Eye Movement Desensitization and Reprocessing (EMDR) is a psychotherapy approach designed to help individuals process and heal from traumatic experiences and distressing memories. EMDR integrates elements of cognitive-behavioral therapy with bilateral stimulation, typically through guided eye movements. During therapy, patients are encouraged to recall traumatic memories while the therapist facilitates bilateral stimulation, which can help reduce the emotional charge associated with those memories. This process aims to reprocess the trauma, allowing patients to develop a more adaptive perspective and diminish symptoms of anxiety, depression, and PTSD. EMDR is recognized for its effectiveness in fostering healing and resilience, enabling individuals to move forward in their lives with greater emotional stability and clarity.

Psychodynamic Psychotherapy

Psychodynamic psychotherapy is a therapeutic approach rooted in the principles of psychoanalysis, emphasizing the exploration of the unconscious mind and the influence of past experiences on present behavior. This form of therapy seeks to uncover and understand underlying psychological conflicts, often stemming from childhood, that shape an individual's thoughts, emotions, and relationships. Through a variety of techniques, therapists help patients gain insight into their internal struggles and unresolved issues. By fostering self-awareness, individuals can work toward healing emotional wounds, improving interpersonal relationships, and achieving greater overall psychological well-being.

Here are a few reflection questions that may help guide your search if you decide to pursue therapy:

- Are you looking for therapy with a structured focus on learning and practicing new skills, or a supportive space to process current events and stressors? The level of structure versus fluidity in therapy varies greatly between different therapeutic approaches and by provider style.
- Are you prepared to and interested in completing between-session work? Some approaches emphasize between-session skills practice, while others do not require much between-session practice.

- To what degree do you feel that your early life experiences and family of origin dynamics are contributing to current distress? Are you interested in exploring the impact of the past on the present, or do you wish primarily for a present-day focus?

Additionally, here are a few questions to help guide you in identifying a therapist that may be well-suited to your needs and preferences:

- How important is it to you that your therapist be experienced in working with first responders or healthcare professionals? Note that your employer may have a list of vetted providers you might consider, and colleagues may have first-hand experience and referrals that could be useful to you. You can also ask providers directly about their experiences with your professional community when you inquire about services.
- Are you hoping to meet with your provider virtually, in person, or both? If you are hoping for sessions in person, narrow your search to providers that practice close enough to where you live so that travel to their office would not be a deterrent from continuing to attend therapy.
- Do you have a preference with regard to a therapist's gender, race, religion, second language knowledge, or other characteristics?
- Finally, consider the personality characteristics you feel would make therapy easiest for you. Some patients prefer a more hands-on therapist who offers concrete guidance and interventions, while others prefer a more open-ended, patient-centered approach. Some patients value an unconditionally compassionate space, while others describe being put off by an effusively warm therapist and explicitly ask to be challenged by their provider.

Many providers offer brief introductory calls before scheduling a session. Do not hesitate to come into these calls prepared with a list of questions and feel free to talk with several therapists to assess how you feel while speaking with them. Notice both what the therapists say, and how comfortable and inclined to share you feel when you are speaking with them.

As you begin therapy, offer your clinician feedback on how the sessions are matching your expectations and how the therapist may best serve you. The more explicit you can be about your needs and preferences, the more likely your provider is to meet them.

Beginning therapy can be intimidating, but therapy can also be enormously rewarding. I hope your journey in therapy is a fruitful one.

CHAPTER 31

Conclusion

As we prepare to wrap up this journey together, you might find yourself having many different thoughts and feelings. You may (I hope!) feel inspired and energized, having discovered some concrete new ways to preserve and enhance your psychological well-being.

I imagine, though, that for many of you, there may be feelings of sadness and discouragement—so many things to process, so many potential changes to make, and perhaps, reading this book has made difficult past experiences come into awareness.

What I have laid out in this book is a broad introduction to the psychological difficulties faced by first responders and healthcare workers, along with strategies to overcome them. The awareness of these is already part of the journey toward change. In particular, I have emphasized how self-compassion, mindfulness practices, and overcoming unhelpful self-talk and avoidant behaviors can greatly increase your sense of well-being. Not all of the sections may have been equally relevant to you, but I hope you found some passages, case examples, and skills worth holding onto and reflecting on further.

Since it is easy to become overwhelmed and discouraged by the volume of content shared, you might consider picking two or three key ideas or tools from the sections that felt most relevant to you and begin bringing them into practice. Start small and set yourself up for experiences of success. This will allow the momentum and motivation to continue to grow.

I hope that for some of you, this book has inspired a willingness to pursue a deeper, richer journey inward with a therapist. I have written this book deliberately using a casual, personal, non-academic tone to give you a taste of the tone and rhythm of what therapy could look like. There are quite a few of us out there now whose careers have focused on caring for the helpers. With the introduction of telemedicine, access to care has improved significantly, and it is possible to have a meaningful journey and experience growth and insights without ever even leaving home.

We healthcare professionals and first responders are often among the first to help others, but the last to seek help for ourselves. Above all else, I hope that this book has helped you consider some new ways of caring for yourself, so you can stay well while serving others. I assure you that it is very possible, though not easy, to thrive despite the stress and heavy demands of first responder and healthcare professions. I hope this book has offered some useful tools and guidance as you find your own way to well-being, despite the personal and professional challenges you may face now and in the future.

Thank you for all you do, and do remember to take care of yourself.

Acknowledgements

I would like to express my sincere gratitude to my dear friends — Vivian, Ivana, Lisa, Shlomo, Dalit, Rachel, and Donna — for their candour, patience, and thoughtful feedback throughout the writing process. Your confidence in me and in this project has been valuable and deeply appreciated.

My thanks also go to Dr. Sarah Meehan O'Callaghan for her editorial guidance, which helped shape my ideas into clear and coherent form. I am equally grateful to Andy Magee and Sabir Hussain for their creativity and inspired design work, which has ensured that the book's presentation reflects the care invested in its content.

References

Alonso-Alonso, M., Woods, S.C., Pelchat, M., Grigson, P.S., Stice, E., Farooqi, S., Khoo, C.S., Mattes, R.D., & Beauchamp, G.K (2015). Food reward system: current perspectives and future research needs. *Nutrition Reviews,* 73(5):296-307.

American Psychiatric Association. (2022). *Diagnostic and statistical manual of mental disorders* (5th ed., text rev.).

Aurelius, M. (2002). *Meditations* (G. Hays, Trans.). *Modern Library.* (Original work published ca. 180 CE)

Bikman, B. (2020). *Why we get sick: The hidden epidemic at the root of most chronic disease—and how to fight it.* BenBella Books.

Black, D. S., & Slavich, G. M. (2016). Mindfulness meditation and the immune system: A systematic review of randomized controlled trials. *Annals of the New York Academy of Sciences, 1373*(1), 13–24.

Blanchette, I. (2006). In harm's way: On preferential response to threatening stimuli. *Cognition and Emotion, 20*(4–6), 1081–1099.

Boivin, D. B., Boudreau, P., & Kosmadopoulos, A. (2021). Disturbance of the circadian system in shift work and its health impact. *Journal of Biological Rhythms, 37*(1), 3–28.

Bryant, R. A. (2013). A systematic review of PTSD prevalence and trajectories in DSM-5 defined trauma-exposed populations: Intentional and non-intentional traumatic events. *PLoS ONE, 8*(4), e59236

Canadian Centre on Substance Use and Addiction. (2022, July 28). Canada's guidance on alcohol and health. https://www.ccsa.ca/en/guidance-tools-resources/

Carek, P. J., Laibstain, S. E., & Carek, S. (2011). Exercise for the treatment of depression and anxiety. *International Journal of Psychiatry in Medicine, 41*(1), 15–28.

Chah, A. (2018). *Everything arises, everything falls away: Teachings on impermanence and the end of suffering* (P. Breiter, Ed.). Shambhala Publications.

Chambers, R., Lo, B. C. Y., & Allen, N. B. (2008). The impact of intensive mindfulness training on attentional control, cognitive style, and affect. *Cognitive Therapy and Research, 32*(3), 303–322.

Cohen, S., Janicki-Deverts, D., & Miller, G. E. (2007). Psychological stress and disease. *JAMA, 298*(14), 1685–1687

Creswell, J. D. (2017). Mindfulness interventions. *Annual Review of Psychology, 68,* 491–516.

Dana, D. (2018). *The polyvagal theory in therapy: Engaging the rhythm of regulation.* W. W. Norton & Company.

The Holy Bible, English Standard Version. (2001). *Ecclesiastes 3:2.* Crossway Bibles.

Frankl, V. E. (1963). *Man's search for meaning: An introduction to logotherapy.* Washington Square Press.

Gantz, F. E., Gallagher-Thompson, D., & Rodman, J. L. (1992). Inhibited grief. In A. Freeman & F. M. Dattilio (Eds.), *Comprehensive Casebook of Cognitive Therapy* (pp. 201–207). Springer.

Golbidi, S., Badran, M., Ayas, N., & Laher, I. (2012). Cardiovascular consequences of sleep apnea. *Lung, 190*(2), 113–132.

Government of Canada. (2019, May 10). *Canada's lower-risk cannabis use guidelines.* https://www.canada.ca/en/health-canada/services/drugs-medication/cannabis/resources/lower-risk-cannabis-use-guidelines.html

Government of Canada. (2024, September 16). *Suicide in Canada.* https://www.canada.ca/en/public-health/services/suicide-prevention/suicide-canada.html

Goyal, M., Singh, S., Sibinga, E. M., Gould, N. F., Rowland-Seymour, A., Sharma, et al. (2014). Meditation programs for psychological stress and well-being: A systematic review and meta-analysis. *JAMA Internal Medicine, 174*(3), 357–368.

Hall, W., & Degenhardt, L. (2008). Understanding comorbidity between cannabis use and psychotic disorders: The role of substance use. *World Psychiatry, 7*(2), 68–71.

Hanh, T. N. (2012). *Anger: Wisdom for cooling the flames.* Parallax Press.

Hanh, T. N. (2002). *No death, no fear: Comforting wisdom for life.* Riverhead Books.

Hanh, T. N. (2002). *True love: A practice for awakening the heart.* Shambhala.

Hanh, T. N. (2009). *The Art of Mindful Living.* Parallax Press.

Hanson, F. (2023, November 6). Using the polyvagal theory for trauma [Video]. *Being Well Podcast.* YouTube. https://www.youtube.com/watch?v=CWVgXQKrqQ4

Hanson, R. (2013). *Hardwiring happiness: The new brain science of contentment, calm, and confidence.* Harmony Books.

Health Canada. (2025, April 2). *Caffeine in foods.* Government of Canada. https://www.canada.ca/en/health-canada/services/food-nutrition/food-safety/food-additives/caffeine-foods.html

Hines, S. E., Chin, K. H., Glick, D. R., & Wickwire, E. M. (2021). Psychiatric symptoms and moral injury among U.S. healthcare workers in the COVID-19 era: A cross-sectional study. *BMC Psychiatry, 21*(1), – 394.

Jones, C., & Gwenin, C. (2020). Cortisol level dysregulation and its prevalence—Is it nature's alarm clock? *Physiological Reports, 8*(24), e14644

Kabat-Zinn, J. (1990). *Full catastrophe living: Using the wisdom of your body and mind to face stress, pain, and illness.* Delta.

Kabat-Zinn, J. (1994). *Wherever you go, there you are: Mindfulness meditation in everyday life.* Hyperion.

Kabat-Zinn, J. (2012). *Mindfulness for beginners: Reclaiming the present moment—and your life.* Sounds True.

Kalanithi, P. (2016). *When breath becomes air.* Random House.

Karimi, L., Leggat, S. G., Bartram, T., Afshari, L., Sarkeshik, S., & Verulava, T. (2021). Emotional intelligence: Predictor of employees' well-being, quality of patient care, and psychological empowerment. *BMC Psychology, 9*(93).

Kashdan, T. B., & Rottenberg, J. (2010). Psychological flexibility as a fundamental aspect of health. *Clinical Psychology Review, 30*(4), 467–480.

Keng, S. L., Smoski, M. J., & Robins, C. J. (2011). Effects of mindfulness

on psychological health: A review of empirical studies. *Clinical Psychology Review, 31*(6), 1041–1056.

Koob, G. F., & Le Moal, M. (2008). Addiction and the brain antireward system. *Annual Review of Psychology, 59*, 29–53.

Kornfield, J. (1993). *A path with heart: A guide through the perils and promises of spiritual life.* Bantam Books.

Kornfield, J. (2008). *The wise heart: A guide to the universal teachings of Buddhist psychology.* Bantam Books.

Kozlowska, K., Walker, P., McLean, L., & Carrive, P. (2015). Fear and the defense cascade: Clinical implications and management. *Harvard Review of Psychiatry, 23*(4), 263–287

Krukowski, J. (2014, August 26). *Achieving your goals: An evidence-based approach.* Michigan State University Extension. https://www.canr.msu.edu/news/achieving_your_goals_an_evidence_based_approach

Lane, M. M., Gamage, E., Du, S., Ashtree, D. N., McGuinness, A. J., Gauci, S., et al. (2024). Ultra-processed food exposure and adverse health outcomes: Umbrella review of epidemiological meta-analyses. *British Medical Journal, 384.*

Lang, P. J. (2000). Fear and anxiety: Animal models and human cognitive psychophysiology. *Journal of Affective Disorders, 61*(3), 137–159.

Lanius, R. A., Harricharan, S., Kearney, B. E., & Pandev-Girard, B. (2025). *Sensory pathways to healing from trauma: Harnessing the brain's capacity for change*. Guilford Press.

Linehan, M. M. (2015). *DBT® Skills Training Manual* (2nd ed.). The Guilford Press.

Litz, B. T., & Walker, H. E. (2025). Moral injury: An overview of conceptual, definitional, assessment, and treatment issues. *Annual Review of Clinical Psychology, 21,* 251-277

Lustig, R. H. (2021). *Metabolical: The lure and the lies of processed food, nutrition, and modern medicine*. HarperWave.

Kaylor, L. (2025). *If sleep were a drug: The science of sleep optimization—Biohack your brain, body, and performance*. Kaylor Books.

Kiloby Center for Recovery. (2017, October 21). *Gabor Maté - Trauma is disconnection from the self* [Video]. YouTube. https://www.youtube.com/watch?v=sG5W1xnOreQ

Maté, G. (2003). *When the body says no: The cost of hidden stress.* A. A. Knopf Canada.

Maté, G., & Maté, D. (2022). *The myth of normal: Trauma, illness, and healing in a toxic culture*. Avery.

Moran, D. J., & Ming, S. (2023). *Finding your why and finding your way: An acceptance and commitment therapy workbook*. New Harbinger Publications.

Neff, K. (2011). *Self-compassion: The proven power of being kind to yourself.* William Morrow.

Neff, K. (n.d.). *Exercise 2: Self-Compassion Break* [Web page]. Self-Compassion.org. https://self-compassion.org/exercises/exercise-2-self-compassion-break/

Neff, K. (n.d.). *Exercise 3: Exploring self-compassion through writing* [Web page]. Self-Compassion.org. https://self-compassion.org/exercises/exercise-3-exploring-self-compassion-through-writing/

Neff, K. D. & Germer, C. (2017). Self-Compassion and Psychological Wellbeing. In J. Doty (Ed.) *Oxford Handbook of Compassion Science,* Chap. 27. Oxford University Press.

Neff, K.D., & Germer, C. (2018). *The Mindful Self-Compassion Workbook: A Proven Way to Accept Yourself, Build Inner Strength, and Thrive.* Guilford Press.

Nietzsche, F. (2008). *Twilight of the idols* (A. Ridley, Trans.). Oxford University Press. (Original work published 1888)

Omidbakhsh Z, Mohammadi Z, & Soltanabadi S. (2025). Childhood Maltreatment and Complex PTSD: A Systematic Literature Review. *Trauma Violence Abuse. 26*(2), 123–145

Palmer, C. M. (2022). *Brain energy: A revolutionary breakthrough in understanding mental health—and improving treatment for anxiety, depression, OCD, PTSD, and more*. BenBella Books.

Plutchik, R. (1980). *Emotion: A psychoevolutionary synthesis.* Harper & Row.

Porges, S. W. (1995). Orienting in a defensive world: Mammalian modifications of our evolutionary heritage: A Polyvagal Theory. *Psychophysiology, 32*(4), 301–318.

Porges, S. W. (2022). Polyvagal Theory: A Science of Safety. *Frontiers in Integrative Neuroscience, 16,* 871227.

Raza, M.L., Haghipanah, M., & Moradikor, N. (2024). Coffee and stress management: How does coffee affect the stress response? *Progress in Brain Research, 288,* 59-80.

Seligman, M. E. P. (2011). *Flourish: A visionary new understanding of happiness and well-being.* Free Press.

Seneca the Younger. (n.d.). *On Providence.* Retrieved from https://www.gutenberg.org/ebooks/10633

Shah, A. J., Vaccarino, V., Goldberg, J., et al. (2024). Posttraumatic stress disorder and obstructive sleep apnea in twins. *JAMA Network Open, 7*(6), e2416352.

Schwartz, R. C. (2021). *No bad parts: Healing trauma and restoring wholeness with the internal family systems model.* Sounds True.

Simon, O.R., Swann, A.C., Powell, K.E., Potter, L.B., Kresnow, M.J., & O'Carroll, P.W. (2001). Characteristics of impulsive suicide attempts and attempters. *Suicide and Life Threatening Behaviour.* 32(1),49-59.

Sorkhou, M., Bedder, R. H., & George, T. P. (2021). The behavioral sequelae of cannabis use in healthy people: A systematic review. *Frontiers in Psychiatry, 12,* Article 630247.

Stockly, L. (2022). *Anger Iceberg.* Creative Play Therapist. https://creativeplaytherapist.com/anger-iceberg/

Sudai, M. (2021). Not dying alone: The need to democratize hospital visitation policies during COVID-19. *Journal of Law and the Biosciences, 8*(2), lsab020.

Tedeschi, R. G., & Calhoun, L. G. (2004). Posttraumatic growth: conceptual foundations and empirical evidence. *Psychological Inquiry.* 15, 1–18.

Tolle, E. (2005). *A new earth: Awakening to your life's purpose.* Dutton.

van der Kolk, B. A. (2014). *The body keeps the score: Brain, mind, and body in the healing of trauma.* Viking.

Whitworth J.A., Williamson P.M., Mangos G., & Kelly J.J. (2006). Cardiovascular consequences of cortisol excess. *Vascular Health and Risk Management, 1*(4), 291–299.

Yalom, I. D. (2008). *Staring at the sun: Being at peace with your own mortality.* Jossey-Bass.

www.ingramcontent.com/pod-product-compliance
Lightning Source LLC
LaVergne TN
LVHW050302210926
848481LV00014BA/607